Disturbing Silence

A look into conflict profile of BTAD

Disturbing Silence

A look into conflict profile of BTAD

Anuradha Dutta
Urmimala Sengupta

AKANSHA PUBLISHING HOUSE
NEW DELHI • GUWAHATI • VISAKHAPATNAM

AKANSHA PUBLISHING HOUSE
4649-B/21, Ansari Road
Darya Ganj, New Delhi - 110 002
Ph.: 23263193 / 9811582579 / 09435116718
Fax: 011-23263193
Email: ektabooks@yahoo.com
www.akanshapublishinghouse.com

Disturbing Silence: A look into conflict profile of BTAD

First Published 2011

ISBN 978-81-8370-256-0

PRINTED IN INDIA

Published by Akansha Publishing House, New Delhi and Printed at Harmain Offset, Delhi.

In memory of Shri Rabindranath Upadhyay who dedicated his life to the place and people of BTAD.

Contents

Preface

The idea of this book was conceived during our first visit to one of the relief camps in BTAD. However, it took us many years to shape the idea in the form of the book. Besides looking at the conflict in BTAD through peace research, a modest attempt has been made through this book to capture the reactions of the civil society members in the area on the issue of inter-community harmony. We have also made an attempt to document the poorly recorded conditions of the conflict-induced internally displaced persons of the area.

We sincerely hope that this book will throw some light on the hitherto neglected issues of the BTAD and bring in necessary changes.

Author

Acknowledgements

While acknowledging the help and support which we received from various quarters, we must begin by thanking National Foundation for India (NFI) for sponsoring the study titled *An initiative for peaceful co-existence: a look into the conflict profile in the Bodo heartland and capacity building needs among the displaced populace in Bodoland Territorial Autonomous District Council* on which this book is based.

We are thankful to Prof. Samir Kumar Das for his remarkable comments on our manuscripts. Our special thanks to Rahul Karmakar, special correspondent, *Hindustan Times* for taking time out of his busy schedule and enriching our work with his valuable suggestions. We would like to record our sincere gratitude to Late Rabindranath Upadhya (for us *Rabin Bhai)* for giving us time out of his busy schedule and conversing with us on gamut of issues concerning BTAD. His knowledge and experience rich comments were a great source of guidance for us.

We are also grateful to the civil society's members (of all the communities) of BTAD who accepted our proposal of beginning a process of dialogue with one another, without these exercises our understanding of the situation would have been incomplete. We would also like to thank our team at Peace Studies, Omeo Kumar Das Institute of Social Change and Development (OKDISCD), Elizabeth Devi, Prateeti

Barman and Afruza Nasrin Islam for their help at various stages of the study. We would like to appreciate the help we received from our librarian at OKDISCD G.B. Devchoudhury and Rustam Ali for the statistical help. Last but not the least we would like to extend our heartfelt gratitude to all the relief camp dwellers who dared to disclose to us their fears and agonies. Without their participation this book would not have seen the light of the day.

Anuradha Dutta
Urmimala Sengupta

1

Introduction

Peace Studies, Omeo Kumar Das Institute of Social Change and Development (OKDISCD) proposed to analyse the situation in the Bodoland Territorial Areas District or BTAD encompassing 3079 villages accross four districts named Baksa, Chirang, Kokrajhar and Udalguri. Like most parts of Assam, the area has a composite population comprising of Bodos, Adivasis, Koch-Rajbonshis, immigrant Muslim, Assamese, Bengali, Nepali and few other groups. History suggests that the inhabitants of BTAD shared a cordial relationship with one another despite ethnic heterogeneity. Through the proposed study, *"An Initiative for Peaceful Co-existence: A Look into the Conflict Profile in the Bodo Heartland and Capacity Building needs among the Displaced Populace in Bodoland Territorial Autonomous District Council, Assam"*, Peace Studies attempted to look into the state of co-existence among the denizens of BTAD, primarily the Bodos, Koch-Rajbangshis, immigrant Muslims and Adivasis.

The term 'coexistence', which was used mostly in International Relations and Political Science disciplines in the 20th century, meant little more than limited peaceful relations between states. Changes ushered in by the new century saw the term being used to refer to a state in which different groups live together by accepting and respecting one another's differences, and more importantly solving their differences amicably. Coexistence that prevailed in BTAD was passive in nature. We call it passive co-existence because the relation between the groups here is marked by unequal power distribution. Though there was no apparent conflict between the communities, social structures were not conducive for social equity and justice.

As researchers we had problem tracing the kind of co-existence that once prevailed between the communities. Our pilot study suggested that the conditions were not encouraging (at the moment) for initiating peaceful coexistence in the study area as misunderstanding leading to mistrust had replaced cooperation and brotherly feelings between the communities. All these factors necessitated a need for change in the course of the research. Therefore, instead of initiating peaceful coexistence, Peace Studies choose to analyse the conflict that had hijacked harmony. Conflict analysis is one of the widely used means to bring back coexistence and peace. Our pilot study also suggested that three conflicts between the Bodos and Koch-Rajbonshis, in 1989, between Bodos and immigrant Muslims in 1993, and between the Bodos and the Adivasis in 1996 and 1998 were very complex in nature. So we restricted ourselves to analysing the conflict between Bodos and Adivasis.

These conflicts led to one question—what determined the Bodos' choice of target one after the other? Civil society organizations like..........organized a chain of protests after the Bodos attacked the Koch-Rajbongshis. Attacks on Muslims invited protests too. Our decision to analyse the Bodos Adivasis conflicts was based on the following:

- The two communities had history of peaceful co-existence.

- Their conflicts affected more people than the other two conflicts.
- The study area witnessed changes in various spheres after the conflicts.

Overview of Bodoland Territorial Area District (BTAD)

Situated in the western part of Assam, Bodoland Territorial Areas District (BTAD) comprises of four districts named Baksa, Chirang, Kokrajhar and Udalguri. Measuring 27,100 km^2 (35%, of Assam)[1], it was carved out of eight existing districts—*Dhubri, Kokrajhar, Bongaigaon, Barpeta, Nalbari, Kamrup, Darrang* and *Sonitpur*.

BTAD happened after a long struggle that began with the Bodoland statehood movement. The All Bodo Students Union (ABSU) and Bodo People's Action Committee (BPAC) launched on March 2, in 1987. The movement sought separate political unit besides, preservation of the language, culture, and ethnic identity of the Bodos, the largest plains tribal group in North-East India.[2]

But, the Bodoland movement turned violent. A series of tripartite talks started under the initiative of the Central government helped check the violence, and on 20 February 1993 a memorandum of settlement (MoS) was signed between the Assam government, ABSU and BPAC. Popularly known as the Bodo Accord *(Annexure I)*, it led to the formation of Bodo Autonomous Council (BAC). The objective of the council as stated in the agreement was to provide maximum autonomy (within the framework of the constitution), to the Bodos for their social, economic, educational, ethnic and cultural advancement. But the accord lacked clarity on certain crucial issues such as the territory of the BAC area. It thus failed to satisfy the non-Bodos as well as a section of Bodos.

Despite this dissatisfaction, BAC continued amid in-house rivalry. The political parties holding the reins of power in

Dispur during that time used this rivalry to gain mileage. Above all, elections to the council were never held. All these in addition to the continued militant activities lead to the signing of another pact on 10 February 2003 in New Delhi. This time the signators were Bodo Liberation Tigers (BLT) chairman Hagrama Basumatary and senior officials of the Union Home Ministry and the state government. *(Annexure II)*.

The new settlement led to the creation of the Bodoland Territorial Council (BTC) within the state of Assam. The area covered under BTC, the administrative organ is known as BTAD. By an amendment of Schedule VI, 40 departments were handed over to the BTC. The BTC was also provided constitutional protection under the Sixth Schedule so that the economic, educational and linguistic aspirations, preservation of land rights, and sociocultural and ethnic identity of the Bodos could be developed. BTC thus made the BAC defunct.

Objectives of the Study

[1]http://en.wikipedia.org/wiki/Bodoland

[2] Chaklader.Snehamoy, (2004), *Sub-Regional movement in India: with reference to Bodoland & Gorkhaland,* K.P. Bhachi & Com, Kolkata.

The prime objective of the study was to analyze the causes of conflict between the Bodos and Adivasis living in BTAD. We felt the urgency/need for such a study mainly due to the following reasons:

- No such attempt was ever made to understand who/what went wrong in the study area, once a trademark of peaceful coexistence.

- Without an understanding of the causes of the conflict, effective steps in the direction of solving the problem cannot be taken.

• Ethnic dominance or control of the administration and politics by a particular group increases the possibility of conflict in future.

The aim of the study is conflict analysis. With this end in mind the following were taken as the objective of the study.

✓ To find out the why/how/when of the Bodo-Advasi conflict.

✓ To find out and build a network with Self Help Groups (SHGs), government organizations, Non-Governmental Organizations (NGOs), Civil Society organizations operational in BTAD toward better coexistence.

✓ To document the conditions of the camp dwellers in the area.

Scope and Limitation

This study is a part of the proposed two year action research. Peace Studies shifted its focus to conflict analysis owing to negative coexistence. In the process of the study we came across cases of trafficking, post - conflict trauma victims, juvenile delinquencies ugly scar left by long drawn conflict in the area. As social scientists we see these as potential fields of research.

As far as limitations are concerned Peace Studies field investigators had to brave natural calamities like flood as well as manmade problems such as *bandhs* (blockade and shutdown). Moreover, it took some time to establish a rapport with the victims of the conflict and ease their hesitation in opening up and speaking about the conflict and other related aspects.

Additionally, it was found that the absence of neutral third party intervention was one of the reasons behind the delay in trust rebuilding process among the conflicting parties.

The sense of relative deprivation was so rampant among the victims that an urgent third party intervention seemed to be the most feasible way to address the problem. To fulfill this objective, a survey was conducted to find out if the victims would prefer to work with neutral but local NGOs or neutal organizations from outside BTAD. For the purpose of pilot study, Kasugaon relief camp was selected. The survey findings reconfirmed that civil society organizations at the local levels were yet to convince the victims of their neutrality, and the preference of intervention of neutral organizations from outside the area was overwhelming. These findings entailed a great responsibility of finding an organization that would volunteer to intervene in the conflict area. After initial disappointments, we came across Society for Promotion of Appropriate Development Efforts (SPADE). This NGO, working on livelihood promotion in rural areas, agreed to be partner in an endeavour to lessen the feeling of relative deprivation among the conflict victims through livelihood enhancement programmes. Before taking up any skill enhancement programme, SPADE wanted to find out how they evaluated their capacity of livelihood before the Entrepreneurship and Skill Development Programmes (ESDPs) were launched. Camp inmates between 18-35 years of age were asked to evaluate themselves on their capacity to earn a livelihood. The following were the findings.

Table 1: Showing a self assessment of capacity for livelihood before the ESDPs were started in the relief camps

Self assessment of capacity of earning a livelihood	*Gender*	*Highly Capable*	*Capable to some extent*	*Not at all capable*	*No opinion*	*Total %*
	Male	7.8%	15.2%	61.6%	15.4%	**100**
	Female	5.5%	23.7%	58.9%	11.9%	**100**

The finding showed that in the case of both males as well as females majority of both the respondents i.e. 61.6 % males and 58.9 % females felt that they lacked capability to earn livelihood. This finding takes us to a natural query as to what according to them is the reason behind their incapability. The following table provides us the answer.

Table 2: Showing reasons behind lack of capacity of earning livelihood

Reasons for incapacity of earning a livelihood	*Gender*	*Lack of knowledge about opportunities of livelihood*	*Lack of capital*	*Lack of adequate skill*	*Cannot say*	*Total %*
	Male	14.6 %	15.2%	67.8%	2.4%	**100**
	Female	15.5%	12.2%	62.3%	10%	**100**

From the above table one can safely say that relief camp inmates differ from the general perception that lack of capital is the major obstacle behind incapability of earning livelihood. According 67.8 % males and 62.3% female respondents, it is lack of skill that makes them incapable of earning a livelihood. Another factor in the way of earning livelihood was lack of adequate information about livelihood options. SPADE was selected cater to the needs of the inmates on the basic of these important findings. SPADE conducted ESDP on bamboo craft in the Kasugaon relief camp in collaboration with Indian Institute of Entrepreneurship (IIE), Guwahati. The ESDP was sponsored by Ministry of Micro, Small, and Medium Enterprises (MSME). In addition to skill development classes the trainees (25 for each ESDP) also had sessions on marketing, accounting and book keeping, motivation etc., keeping in mind the fact that most of the EDPS applicants were school dropouts. The courses were designed as simple as possible. To empirically verify if there was any impact of the ESDPs, the same respondents who were asked to assess their capacity for livelihood before the capacity building training camps were asked to reassess themselves after the completion of the programme. Table 3 shows the finding of the re-assessment.

Table 3: Showing a self assessment of capacity for livelihood after the ESDPs were started in the relief camps

Self assessment of capacity of earning a livelihood	*Gender*	*Highly Capable*	*Capable to some extent*	*Not at all capable*	*No opinion*	*Total %*
	Male	11.6%	26.2%	49.9%	12.3%	**100**
	Female	8.4%	38.9%	43.4%	9.3%	**100**

The table shows a considerable leap in the confidence level of the camp inmates after the completion of the ESDPs. Post-ESDPs, 26.2% males felt they were capable to some extent to earn a livelihood as compared to 15.2% males earlier. The percentage of those who felt incapable of earning livelihood also dipped after the ESDPs. All these indicate that the ESDPs boosted the confidence level of the relief camp inmates. Therefore, SPADE plans to continue its 'handholding programme' until some of the trainees establish their own enterprise individually or collectively. Here it needs to be mentioned that such programmes would not have been possible with the government's support. If this model of NGO intervention is followed in all the relief camps the issue of relative deprivation can be addressed to a considerable level. And this will go a long way in reestablishing the trust and harmony once prevalent in area. However, since the issue involves tens of thousands of people it is not possible for NGOs alone to come up with such programmes. Therefore sustained interest of government agencies (as was shown in this case) is a necessity.

2

Introducing Peace Research

Understanding evolution of the concept of peace *per se* will help know and appreciate the need for peace research. Renaissance humanism of the 18th century for the first time broadens the idea of peace. From then on peace meant more than cessation of wars it began to be viewed as a way to realizing social justice, freedom, improvement and development of life.[1] This broad idea of peace is perhaps responsible for the age-old tension that existed between peace and justice. Years later, this tension transformed into two acceptable distinctions: negative peace and positive peace. While negative peace means absence of all forms of violent (overt) conflicts, positive peace has a wider meaning. Apart from cessation of violent, it means a social system marked by positive elements such as coexistence, cohesion, it also pertains to a society that has attained maturity for constructive resolution of conflicts.

Prior to 1945 peace hardly found any academic attention. Individuals like M.K. Gandhi, Q. Wright and L.F. Richardson contributed immensely to peace during this period. But more noteworthy is Johan Galtung's pioneering effort since 1945 in the field of peace science, peace education, peace research and peace studies. To Galtung, peace research, was as old as humankind, but it took long for the discipline to affirm itself. Galtung was also of the opinion that 'definition imposition on a growing field may all too easily prove detrimental to its development.'[2]

Peace research seeks to understand the cause(s) behind a given conflict besides unearthing prospects for peace. In other words a peace researcher not only traces the causes of a given turmoil in the pages of history, she is also concerned about its present implications and how to transform the conflict into peace in the future. There have been several attempts at various conferences to define peace research. One such attempt was made by Katsuya Kodama, Secretary General of International Peace Research Association (IPRA). He said, "Peace research has grown out of hard reflection on the tragedies of the Second World War and out of worry about the nuclear weapons competition between the United States and the Soviet Union which so rapidly advanced during the following years."[3] As such, the focus of peace research in the post-World War II period was on various forms of conflict between the major nations. During this phase peace research was essentially looking for ways to prevent future wars between nations. The scope of peace research was thus narrow. But peace research gradually shifted its attention to the changing realities of the world. A survey (which included more then 100 peace and conflict research institutes) conducted on attitudes towards positive and negative peace is indicative of the changing trend of peace research. It revealed that a majority (44%) of them felt that peace research should shift its focus to positive peace while 28% of the institutions opined that positive peace should at least be a part of peace research.[4] Helena Rytovuori observes, that the movement from ideational to the enthropo-centric conception has been instrumental in shaping our concept of peace research.[5]As has been pointed out by Mohammed Ahsen

Chaudhuri peace research lacks precision and clarity. To a certain extent the changing perception of peace is responsible for lack of unanimity regarding the definition of peace research. Despite these shortcomings the first conference of IPRA revealed the following characteristics of peace research:

- Both study of conflict as well as co-operation between states and within states fall under the ambit of peace research.

- Peace research is an attempt to alternatives to war/violence by finding out conditions for peace through scholarly research.

- Negating the claims, made by some that peace research has a greater tilt towards international relation, the conference held the view that the subject is interdisciplinary, i.e., all established academic disciplines can take part in it.[6]

Giving due respect to the above objectives of peace research, here an attempt has been made not to restrict our attention to the whys of violent conflicts. Possible ways of reviving the co-operation and co-existence that existed between Bodos and Adivasis have also been attended to. Under the present situation (BTAD) where the patient (the society therein) is undergoing multiple organ disorder (various problems like inter - ethnic tension, gross underdevelopment of some sections of the society etc.) and the objective is complete cure, knowledge of various disciplines comes handy. Luc Reychler has aptly explained why it is necessary for peace research to be interdisciplinary in character. The scholar views peace building as an inclusive effort that requires the knowledge of economist, lawyer, political scientist, psychologist, educators, theologians and others. And as peace research and its findings play important role in peace building, peace researchers are suggested to transform their "narrow narcissism into productive narcissism by inviting all to play in the orchestra of peace building".[7]

Another important feature of peace research is that it deals with 'sentimental' walls, viz., theories, assumptions, expectations, attitudes, feelings, taboos, beliefs, norms and principles that stand in the way of conflict prevention and peace building.[8] This feature of peace research is very appealing to the situation of Northeast and Jammu and Kashmir where 'sentimental' issues such as 'feeling of alienation' and 'step child syndrome' form a part and parcel of the society but these issues more than often either escape the notice of researchers or do not get their due attention.

Apart from the definition another important aspect of peace research is the lack of unanimity in conducting it. Though there is a plethora of research methodology, the choice is limited when it comes to applying them to peace research. In fact, the discipline is yet to have an integrated scientific method of investigation. Amidst these limitations historical-analytical, mathematical approach, model building, empirical analytical, interpretative, peace action research and observation are some methods used in carrying out peace research. But most of these methods have serious flaws. For instance, the classical historical analytical method that mostly involves a single scholar taking unsystematic notes of 'relatively implicit criteria',[9] interprets in an unscientific manner is less likely to be useful to the customers of peace research. Mathematical and model building methods are also faulty. A peace researcher who applies these methods to her problem is most likely to look at it technically, and this approach is against the objective of peace research. However, interpretative, peace action research and to some extent observation methods find more acceptability among peace researchers.

Peace action research that sees ordinary men and women as an active subjects of research and believes that they have a universal right to participate in the production of knowledge which affects them (and in some cases which is about them), is gradually gaining popularity. The critique of research methodology should give due consideration to the fact that when action takes over, scientific aspects tends to take a back seat.[10] Moreover three types of observation methods—projective thinking, goal thinking and policy thinking have the potential of helping peace researchers to get to their goals. But Mohammed Ahsen Chaudhuri laments the fact that instead of considering the observation method that is most likely to help a researcher attain the instrumentalist, contextual and consequential research goals, she prefers to take the most traveled road - building a theory of peace in the light of her own discipline.[11]

Perhaps the over-consciousness on the part of peace researchers to be 'scientific' in their research method lure them to take the course of model-building and/or theory building. Unfortunately such temptation many a time drives the researcher away from 'truth'. Additionally in this part of the world, most researchers are obsessed with western theoretical model that can often fail to explain the complexities of local porblems. Therefore, while making the choice of methodology, a peace researcher needs to be cautious so that her obsession with research methodology does not drive her away from her goal. It will be in her interest to hold back her obsession for methodology and instead allow the research problem to determine the method. Moreover it is important not to compromise with local uniqueness of local problems while looking at issues through the lenses of western theories.

Along with Japan and the world beyond, peace research has begun to be considered in India too. Peace research in India mostly concentrated on Gandhian perceptions and concerns, and to some extent on the legacy of Gandhian organization and the internal tensions of Indian development.[12] Gandhian organizations have been working for peace in this region too. Tamulpur Anchalik Gramdan Sangh (TAGS) is one such organization located at

Kumarikata in the Baksa district of Assam. Founded in 1962, by Late Ravindra Nath Upadhyaya, who believed in positive peace,TAGS has been working in the area on various programmes such as:

- Production of Khadi, mustard oil, bee-keeping boxes
- Community Development, (malaria eradication) health and women empowerment through SHGs.
- Relief Work for victims of natural as well as man-made calamities
- Programmes Specifically Aimed at sensitization and mobilization through peace education,training and action.

However, conflict prone pockets such as Jammu and Kashmir and most parts of the Northeast have not seen much in terms of peace research. The subject is yet to make its need a necessity in India.

Why we need Peace Research?

India's journey of nation-building began by incorporating princely states and other geographical units such as the 'Northeast'. But unlike the princely states that were for long part of colonial India, the northeastern frontier (term coined by the British regime) came under the colonial rule only after 1826. It is argued by many that during the euphoric phase of nation-building the makers of the India wished to include as many princely states and other geographical units as was possible. This exercise was rather whimsical it was often felt that the "Indian state was by and large groping in the dark for it did not know for certain what the constituent elements of the nation would be...".[13] As a result of this constitution of India became an 'ensemble of accords'[14]. In the process of pursing accords, the nation was split into two asymmetrical spheres – the civilized and the uncivilized. The civilized sphere consists of those societies that have the potential of striking deal with the state, those without such potentials were in the uncivilized sphere. Here, our attention is devoted towards the so called 'uncivilized' sphere, i.e., the northeast.

Northeast became a part of India without the singing of any formal treaty. Even strong protest against integration with the Indian state by the Nagas was not handled with care. In fact the treatment meted out to the Nagas by the government implied that "they do not enjoy any right to be consulted or taken into confidence."[15] All these sowed a sense of alienation among the Nagas. In the subsequent phase little effort was made by the Indian state to undo the sense of alienation among the Nagas, instead the policy stand of the Indian state led to a widespread sense of alienation in the entire region.

People of Assam for long had to struggle, adopting themselves to the policies of independent India. The unfortunate gap between mainland India and undivided Assam, which then included Meghalaya, Mizoram, Nagaland and Arunachal Pradesh was well captured in the words of Lokopriya Gopinath Bordoloi, in 1949: He lamented:

> "I feel that I cannot congratulate you when some of you seem to say that you know so little of Assam. Assam is a great part of this country—beautiful and wealthy in all that nature has given but poor and neglected in all that man has done. But I feel, if even today you begin to take an active interest in this part of India and her simple and unsophisticated people, much will grow and develop there for which you will have reasons to be proud and happy. In this busy world of today we hardly have time enough to look around and those who have it are engrossed with what is close at hand. Therefore, the beauty of looking at a thing as it is, the glory of helping one of your own brother and neighbour is lost sight of. Yet, not so were your forefathers centuries and centuries ago and I can tell you that Assam, then known as Pragjothish or Kamrupa, and her people even from pre-historic times were better known to the rest of India than you seem to know your successors."[16]

Even such sentiments were not enough to grab the attention of policy makers, who continued with their 'discriminatory', stand towards Assam and rest of the region. In the post-independent era, industry, transport and banking sectors in Assam remained underdeveloped. Moreover, New Delhi gave Assam less than 35% of the value as royalty despite contibuting 60% of India's crude oil production. Sectors such as tea and plywood were similarly neglected as well. Such discriminations alongside policy indifference towards illegal migration from neighboring Bangladesh, which became a major threat to the state and its people, made grounds fertile for a mass movement in 1979 under the leadership of All Assam Students' Union or AASU.

The movement ended with the signing of the Assam accord in 1985. However, unlike the Assam movement that was brought to a halt before turning violent, this was not so in case of other movements that took place in the region. One of the most popular means adopted by certain groups in this region to register protest against the Indian state has been through armed movements. Over the years the violent armed movements became synonym with the Northeast.

This trouble torn region has managed to grab attention of scholars from across the length and breadth of the nation and beyond. But in most cases the scholarly attention is restricted to a historical analysis of the problems faced by the region. Since it is not possible to deal with the region in its entirety, we shall concentrate on Assam in general and on BTAD in particular. For example, in case of Assam (the second largest state in the region) the upsurge of ULFA movement, the Bodoland movement and various inter-ethnic conflicts have been (mostly) studied within the historical and identity framework.

Scholars like H.K. Barpujari and Udayon Misra have traced the quest for ethnic upsurge and secession to major historical events of the state. While there is no denying the fact that historical perspective is crucial to understanding the complexities of the turmoil in the state, dealing with the issue exclusively from a historical framework limits one's insight into the impending events. Therefore, in addition to historical perspective, conflict analysis paradigm comes handy for a complete understanding of any given conflict. Conflict analysis approach that entails probing all aspects of a given conflict gives due importance to historical aspects while enabling enquiry into the causes of conflict beyond the historical paradigm. Quite naturally, the flexibility of the conflict analysis approach scares high with peace researchers. But conflict analysis alone cannot solve the problem, there is a need for a mechanism that has the potential of transforming violent conflicts into prospects for peace.

Given the fact that peace research goes beyond finding the causes of the conflict, one of its crux areas is suggesting effective policy reform. Peace research seems to be the way out, but invarably not applied to the state. Whatever research has been done on violent conflicts in India is merely from the perspective of conflict research. Over the years this line of research has more harm than good, such exercise diagnoses the sores but leaves the wound untreated. And without effective prescription, there can be no cure. In the absence of proper diagnosis of the causes of the violent conflict(s) followed by practical suggestions to solve them there is every possibility that the conflicts will persist. It is here that peace research can serve both the purposes – to find out the cause(s) of a given discord and accordingly suggest its peaceful solution.

Applicability of peace research in BTAD

The BTAD area has witnessed several phases of conflict. The first one started in 1989 between the Bodos and the Koch-Rajbongshis. In 1993, immigrant Muslims bore the brunt of Bodo hatred. The third and the most brutal of clashes between the Bodos and non-Bodos took place in the May 1996 and again in 1998. Bodos-Muslims clash erupted again in Udalguri district in October 2008, leaving more than 50 people dead and displacing 80,000. It is believed to have started from a trivial case theft of cattle and poultry. Some reports suggested the cause was the unfurling of the Pakistani flag at Mohanpur in Udalguri.

Ethnic violence how troubled other parts of Assam too such as Karbi Anglong and North Cachar Hills (now Dima Hasao). There is the issue of the outlawed United Liberation Front of Assam that has been waging a war against the Indian Union since 1979. Assam nevertheless is yet to see the application of peace research to various forms of violence she has been facing over the years. There are studies on conflicts in BTAD such as the one by Shusheela Bhan. But the problems of BTAD are yet to be examined from the perspective of peace research. We have made an attempt to do that in the following chapters.

FOOTNOTES

1. Kende, Istvan, "The History of Peace: Concept and Organisations from the late Middle Ages to the 1870s", in *Journal of Peace Research*, Vol.26,No. 3 (Aug.1989) p-236.

2 Chaudhuri, Mohammed Ahsen, in "Peace Research and the Developing Countries", cited in http://www.jstor.org/stable/422470 Accessed on 24.12.2008

3. Kodama, Katsuya, in "The IPRA Path", cited in http://soc.kuleuven.be/iieb/ipraweb/documents/iprapath.pdf Accessed on 26.2.2009

4. Everts, Philip P., "Development and trends in Peace and Conflict Research,1965-1971: A Survey of Institutions in journal of Conflict Resolution,Vol.16 No.4 p-504 cited in http://www.jstor.org/stable/173536 Accessed on 24.12.2009.

5. Rytovuori, Helena, "Peace Research as 'International" P-285 cited in http://www.jstor.org/stable/423471 Accessed on 24.12.2009.

6. Chaudhuri, Mohammed Ahsen, in "Peace Research and the Developing Countries", *Journal of Peace Research,* Vol. 5, No. 4 (1968), cited in http://www.jstor.org/stable/422470 accessed on 24.12.2008.

7. Reychler, Luc in "Challenges to Peace Research", *International Journal of Peace Studies,* Volume 11, Number 1, Spring/Summer 2006.

8. *Ibid.*

9. Singer, J.David, "Peace Research and Peace Action" in *Bulletin of Atomic Scientist,* January 1963.

10. *Ibid.*

11. Chaudhuri, Mohammed Ahsen, in "Peace Research and the Developing Countries", Journal of Peace Research, Vol. 5, No. 4 (1968), cited in http://www.jstor.org/stable/422470

12. Chatfield,Charles, "International Peace Research: The Field Defined by Dissemination", in Journal of Peace Research, Vol. 16, No. 2 (1979), Sage Publications, Ltd. p-166 Cited in http://www.jstor.org/stable/423710

13. Das, Samir Kumar, "Nobody's Communiqué : Ethnic Accords in North-eastern India", in Das, Samir Kumar (ed), Sage, New Delhi Peace Processes and Peace Accords, p.124.

14. *Ibid.*

15. *Ibid.*

16. Joshi, Mahesh (1981), *Assam: The Indian Conflict,* Prachi Prakashan, New Delhi, p.62.

3

Understanding the Conflict

1.1 Meaning of Conflict

Oxford Advanced Learner's Dictionary defines conflict as serious disagreement; an argument, a struggle; a fight. Conflict also means: to come into collision, be in mutual opposition, clash and to battle, to struggle.[1]

Conflict is understood as 'struggle over values and claims to scarce status, power and resources'. In the broader context, it can be described as disagreement or unpleasantries arising between social actors.[2] Again, when individuals, communities, national, international or regional actors harbor ideas, desires and wants which due to miscommunication, misperception or otherwise is opposed to those of their counterpart, leaving no room for further communication or compromise, the under-stated situation may lead to a series of unpleasant and many a times violent chains of actions and reactions. Such a phenomenon may also be dubbed as conflict.

The above meaning leaves us with an impression that conflict is ubiquitous and occurs at various levels. Thus we see that conflicts form a part and parcel of social relations. Conflict play an important role in bringing positive social change too. Ways of expressing conflict can be violent or non-violent. At times, it is the choice (made by the parties) of using arms that makes the originally non-violent conflict: a violent one.[3]

After the fall of iron curtains the world has witnessed an upward trend in violent conflicts. United Nations Development Programme's (UNDP) Human Development Report, 2005 "International cooperation at a crossroads: Aid, trade and security in an unequal world", reads, "The century that just ended was the most violent humanity has experienced. Nearly three times as many people were killed in conflict in the 20th Century as in the previous four centuries combined."

The report also underscores the changing nature of conflict–from inter-state wars but intra-state struggles. The changing trends of conflict, in the recent past, made grounds fertile for conflict analysis. The following section will give a clear picture of what conflict analysis actually mean.

1.2 What is conflict analysis?

Analyzing conflict is a comprehensive enquiry followed by an understanding of all aspects of a given strife. Broadly speaking conflict analysis is the "systematic study of the profile, causes, actors, and dynamics of conflict" [4] Conflict analysis is one of the best known steps taken for bringing in peace. However, conflict analysis does not end with merely understanding the dynamics, shapes, forms and effects of a given struggle. It also needs to pay attention to the forms of behaviors, the history of the conflicting parties, their interests and needs. Suggestions to end the turmoil make the analysis of conflict complete.

There are a number of approaches or patterns that can be used in analyzing conflict. The approach here involves three steps—analysis of key conflict factors, actor analysis and analysis of capacities for peace.

It is only for the purpose of convenience that the entire analysis has been so divided. In actuality they are closely knitted and therefore needs to be viewed as a whole.

Step 1: Analysis of key conflict factors

This stage all the factors that had a possible role in the conflict. Factors are likely to add to escalation of present tension to violent conflict have also been attended to.

Step 2: Actor analysis

Here, actors refer to all who were involved in the conflict as well as its victims. It may be an individual, a community as a whole or a part of the community or any organization.

Step 3: Analysis of capacities for peace

"Capacities for peace" refers to those structures, processes, means and organizations of the society that works towards the attainment of peace in the society. Here, both formal as well as informal efforts made toward restoring peace in the post-conflict situation have been dealt with.

Step 1

At some point of time communities such as Bodos and Adivasis coexisting peacefully and collaboratively in the present day BTAD. But since their relationship underwent a negative change from the 1990's, they clashed twice, in 1996 and 1998. The path from existence in peace to existence in conflict among these communities is rather blurred. The precipitation of ethnic conflict from a situation of ethnic diversity to a conflicting one is rather complex. The following analysis is an attempt at unearthing the causes behind these conflicts.

1.3 Theorizing the causes of conflict

There are various schools of thoughts explaining the causes of ethnic conflict. Some of them are – (a) Primordial,

(b) Instrumental, (c) Structural, and (d) Constructivist. The last three theories of ethnic conflict seem best suited for explaining the ethnic conflict in hand.

The instrumentalist school of thought seeks to explain ethnic conflicts as an outcome of the actions of group leader, "who use their cultural group as sites of mass mobilizations and as constituencies in their competition for power and resources, because they find them more effective than social classes".[6] Such power crazy leaders meet with success because ethnic groups are more than often than not subjected to, a prolong wait for fulfillment of their long-standing demands. Sunita Parikh also maintains "ethnic attachments were used instrumentally by the elites to further their own goals".[7]

The applicability of this theory in the Bodo-Adivasi conflict can be justified, for it was the elites among the Bodos who mooted the idea of a separate identity. The formation of Plain Tribes Council of Assam in 1967 and the launching of the Bodo movement in 1987 testify their quest for achieving their goals. The Bodo leadership (mis)used ethnicity as a means to achieving their goals. As Ganesh Murmu an inmate of Kasugaon relief camp said: "not only Adivasis, all other non-Bodo groups supported the movement for Bodoland but in return they harassed and kill the non-Bodos. Only the leaders have gained, common people like us have lost everything". A memorandum submitted to Justice Haque Commission by Adivasi Seva Samity, Central Committee (ASS/CC) also suggested that non-Bodos lent their support to the Bodoland movement. (Annexure III).

The exponents of structural approach believe the structural properties that finds expressions in principles of organization often control the patterns of distribution of social hierarchy, power etc. Since the distribution machinery of society is plagued with inequality and discrimination, those who are at the receiving end harbour a feeling of neglect and deprivation. When such feelings are shared by a large number of individuals of the deprived category, they often take recourse to political action. And when constitutional means become ineffective, these people do not hesitate to take up arms and spark off a violent struggle.[8] Iniquitous state patronage to one group through constitutional or institutional arrangements can also play a crucial role in making grounds fertile for ethnic conflict.

The structural theory provides a plausible explanation of the ethnic conflict in BTAD. At one point of time, when the power relations between Bodos and Adivasis was more or less symmetrical, there prevailed mutual trust and coexistence among them. However, the signing of the Bodoland Accord on 20 February 1993, leading to the creation of BAC, sowed the germs of uneven power relation. The Bodos began to regard the Adivasis and the other non-Bodos as a 'stumbling block in the way of inclusion of proposed villages into the BAC. Consequently, the Bodos opted for ethnic cleansing. Similarly in the wake of the increasing socioeconomic inequality and insecurity, the Adivasis choose not to remain silent victims and retaliated making things graver.

The Constructivist school of thought believe that ethnicity by itself cannot be the cause of ethnic conflict. It is the mismanagement of diversity coupled with the failure on the part of the state to craft out an accommodative policy in accordance with the diversity of the place that ultimately results in ethnic conflict. In this case too, peaceful coexistence prevailed until the launching of the Bodo movement (which again points at flawed accommodative policy of the government). In an attempt to contain the Bodo movement which by the early 90s had become a violent one, the government proposed the Bodo Accord. This Accord signed in Kokrajhar, provided for the creation of BAC. But the government failed to arrive at any consensus, on the boundary of BAC and proposed the inclusion of only those villages in which 50% of the inhabitants were Bodos. Instead of containing the Bodoland movement, the formula for creation of BAC added a new dimension to the Bodoland movement and became one of the main causes of the conflict. It was a case of senseless handling of ethnicity, the Bodo-Adivasis clash was the handwork of "state's cultivated politics of difference".

1.4 Immediate cause

In course of our field visits to the area, we had besides relief camp dwellers interacted with the representatives of various organizations including students' organization, women organization etc., belonging to Bodo, Adivasi and immigrant Muslim(s). The initiative was rather discouraged many, feared that the inter-community dialogue forum might add to the tension existing in the area. However, our experience of organizing such a forum in conflict prone areas (North Cachar Hills and Karbi Anglong), with similar situation, did not deter us from organizing the meet. On the day of the meeting we were pleased to find most of our invitees turning up. But, the tension among the groups was palpable. It took us long to make the two groups comfortable in each others company. As the discussion proceeded certain aspects of the clashes were been unveiled. A section of Bodo youth tried to root the conflicts in the unjust treatment that was meted out to one of the prominent leaders of Assam movement— Upendra Brahma. They alleged that the mainstream Assamese society used Bodos and did not give them their dues, owing to which the Bodos had to launch the movement for Bodoland. Interestingly, similar sentiments were expressed by leaders of All Adivasi Students Association of Assam (AATSA). According to them, the Bodos 'used them' in various stages of Bodoland movement, but they deliberately forgot to share the harvest of the movement (indicating at the newly earned autonomy, which brought along special packages). Amidst all the differences of opinion, there was some degree of consensus only one issue—months before the conflicts took place the feeling of alienation, neglect, fear of losing the hard earned autonomy had plagued the minds of both Bodos and Adivasis. And their pent up feelings erupted with the discovery of the bodies of three girls at Satyapur under Gossaigaon police station. These mysterious bodies became the immediate cause of the conflict between the Bodos and the Adivasis. Majority believed the killings of the three girls triggered the conflics, but here too opinions differ on issues such as the identity of the girls, the instigator of the crime etc. An attempt has been made to present different versions of the immediate cause of the conflict, in the following section.

Under the title *"Regarding ethnic clashes between Bodos and Santhals in Assam"*[9] (Adivasis is the umbrella term used to refer to groups such as Santhals, Orangs, Mundas etc., Santhalis being the largest constituent) the issue was discussed in the Lok Sabha. And responding to the various queries regarding the conflict, the then union home minister Murli Manohar Joshi stated that police tried to identify the deceased, but failed. Moreover, political tension prevailed in Assam at that time. Joshi also added that there were wild rumours of Santhals killing the three Bodo girls, which led the inter-community conflict. Though the identity of the girls remained a mystery, they were taken to be Bodos because of the *dokhna* (a traditional dress of Bodo women) their bodies were droped in. And as Satyapur is a Santhal dominated area, there were rumors that the girls were killed by Santhals.

However, Adivasi Cobra Militants of Assam (ACMA) claims that those three girls were prostitutes and were killed to spark off violent clashes between the two communities. Bosco Chermako, Chief organizing Secretary of *All Adivasi Students' Association of Assam* (AASAA) too holds similar opinion. According to him on 8 May, 1996, two Nepali girls and a Bodo girl were brought and kept in a line hotel owned by some Billa Brahma. These girls, dressed in *dokhona,* were killed after being raped. And their dead bodies were left under a culvert near a Santhali village. Arrests followed (eminent persons of Santhal community in Gossaigaon area were arrested as suspects of the mentioned crimes).[10] On the other hand, the bodies of these girls were allowed to rot under the culvert on the pretext of awaiting identification. Owing to this the postmortem failed to reveal the actual identity of the girls.

As already mentioned, though the identity of the girls remained a mystery, since the deceased were clad in *dokhona;* therefore they were regarded as Bodo girls. And as Satyapur is a Santhal dominated area, there were rumors that the girls were killed by Santhals. This incident agitated the Bodos to the extent that they avenged series of violent revenge on the members of Adivasi community. Adivasis also retaliated, these made things graver.

The news spread and agitated Bodos tried to avenge the death of the three supposedly Bodo girls. The Adivasis retaliated. The state administration failed to check the situation from escalating.[11]

1.5 Proximate conflict factors

Proximate factors of conflict are those factors that are "likely to contribute to a climate conducive to violent conflict".[12]

Presently the study area is free from any violent conflict. But the two communities have a long way to go before they return to the kind of mutual peace and harmony they enjoyed in the past. There are several unattended issues; that have the potential of leading the two communities to future turmoil. Among the many issues, the problem of unequal development that stands out. As Chermako put it, "we have only two representatives and they are merely 'puppets' in the hands of the other executive members".

After the formation of BTAD the political power seems to have become monopoly of only one community. As a result of this the other communities harbour a feeling of neglect. These people also allege the BTAD government of discriminatory. In this context the dissatisfaction regarding the issue of rehabilitation of Adivasi camp dwellers was found to be rampant. The dissatisfaction has gone to such a level that an inmate of Bangtol Veterinary Complex camp said "we will come out with *dao* (machete) if anyone comes to ask for votes this time."

While most of the Bodo camp dwellers have been rehabilitated, many Adivasis are awaiting rehabilitation. Apart from administrative hurdles the inmates of the camps are yet to regain their trust on other communities. As a result most of relief camp dwellers in BTAD are languishing for more than a decade now.

In addition to the above, the narratives explaining all the aspects of the conflict which included the reasoning (which is mostly biased) of the conflict, role as well as the effect of the conflict on the community as a whole, the effect of the conflict on the family or on any individual of the family is transmitted from one generation to the other.[13] Such practices are for cultivation of negative feelings against the 'other community'. This view of Gabriel Salomon is applicable in this area too. Here, the trends of socialization can be said to have taken a U-turn from the amity of past. Today the healthy socialization process has been replaced by the seeds of hatred sown in the impressive minds of the youth, through the painful narratives by members of less fortunate community. Such collective as well as individual memories and narratives of conflict, ensures, that the community does not forget (the violent conflict) and forgive (those whom they regard as guilty). The new generation on the other hand has little reasons to disbelief their elders as they themselves are experiencing many problems in the form of improper education and livelihood options. All these are giving reason to the new generation (of the deprived community) to nurture the culture of negative feeling and hatred for their more fortunate counterparts.

Under the above stated circumstances the chances of tension between the two communities graduating to violent conflict looms large.

Step 2

The complexities of conflict often pose an impediment in analyzing the actors of the conflict, in this case too we confronted with similar challenge. A variety of actors who seemed to hold stake in the BTAD, conflicts can be broadly, categorized into two groups—overt stakeholders and covert stakeholders. Overt stakeholders are those who allegedly had direct links with the conflicts and covert stakeholders or back seat driver(s) are those who shielded their identity.

A belief rampant in Adivasi relief camps is that the National Democratic Front of Bodoland (NDFB) is key actors in these conflicts. However, journalist Subir Bhaumik throws some light on the involvement of the Bodo militant leaders in the ethnic conflict. According to Bhaumik one of the military wing chief of NDFB said that they would 'create a majority even if we do not have one because this is our land and [it] cannot go to anyone else'.[14] Moreover, all the civil society members, ex- MLA Charan Nurzary, member of Bodo Sahitya Sabha and others whom we interviewed hesitated to point out who the direct actors were. In such a situation where we do not have enough data, and the few that we have are vague, we are left with very limited options.

In the absences of any empirical evidences to support or reject the claims of the Adivasi camp dwellers, we organized dialogue sessions for finding out the possible involvement of NDFB, or any other groups in the conflict. In most of the dialogue sessions we came across more allegations than truth. The Bodos alleged that the entire Advasi community was involved in the conflict, and not some armed group. According to them every Adivasi household was preparing before the actual outbreak of the conflict. Additionally, when we delved into greater details, we found that the local administration hardly took measures to prevent the escalation of the conflict. Dwellers of Bismuri relief camps even alleged that the police arrived late despite prior information of attacks by armed groups. As far as the Bodo community is concerned, it seems that the issue concerning the 'territory of BAC' (explained in details elsewhere in the book) disturbed them the most. While for Adivasis, their sidelining by the politically empowered 'other group', was a breach of promise by the 'other group'.

Step 3

Several Peace committees were constituted in the conflict affected areas of BTAD. The Kokrajhar Zilla Bibhinna Bhashik Sahitya Sabha Santi Samannoy Abhijan Samity was one such peace efforts. This committee was constituted at a joint convention of the Kokrajhar District Committee of the Assam Sahitya Sabha, the Bodo Sahitya Sabha and Natun Sahitya Parishad. The local church also organized special prayer sessions which included lectures on peace and tolerance. Besides, there were many informal meetings held at the village levels where the villagers were urged not to react to rumours and instead transmit the message of peace, friendship and love. However it was found that such type of peace meetings did not sustain for long. And in most cases there was hardly any follow up programmes. As in most cases of violent conflict in Northeast India, here too flying visits were made by politicians, bureaucrats, academicians, social activists as well as Gandhians immediately after the conflict. But none of them analysed the cause(s) of the conflict, there were hardly any initiatives for organizing a sustained dialogue process between the conflicting groups.

The repetition of conflicts on the lines of ethnicity in the area is a pointer that the peace efforts were perhaps not adequate. Moreover, there is a need for sustained efforts of peace and it needs to be viewed not merely as a 'post-conflict' activity but as an "effort to strengthen the prospect for internal peace and decrease the likelihood of violent conflict..."[15] in future as well.

Understanding the Conflict the Galtung Way

Noted scholar Johan Galtung has developed the *conflict triangle* model that displays the interplay of three factors which has the potential of becoming cause of a given conflict. In the triangle, **A** refers to the certain attitudes of the actors such as hate and fear. **B** refers to behavior of the actor, i.e., whether they pursuit conflict through violent means or they take recourse to peaceful means for reconciliation and solution. **C** is a pointer to the fundamental structural problems in society like unequal access to resources like land or forest resources, lack of political power, etc.

As per the above model a given conflict can start from any corner. In the case of Bodo - Adivasi conflict it is possible that the fear of the Bodos (corner **A** in the triangle) of being outnumbered by the Adivasis in certain areas, owing to which their expected territorial areas could not be brought under the BAC, germinated the seeds of hatred against their long time Adivasi friends. These attitudinal changes from trust to mistrust, from love to hatred, from friendship to fear were exploited by such stakeholders as political and community leaders in order to draw certain selfish benefits. As there were hardly any efforts towards checking of negative attitudes, violent behavior was aroused (corner **B**). In the above mentioned process the structural inequalities (corner **C**) which were more or less accepted by the less fortunate community, began to give a rethought to the iniquitous structure of the society. Until now the two communities were

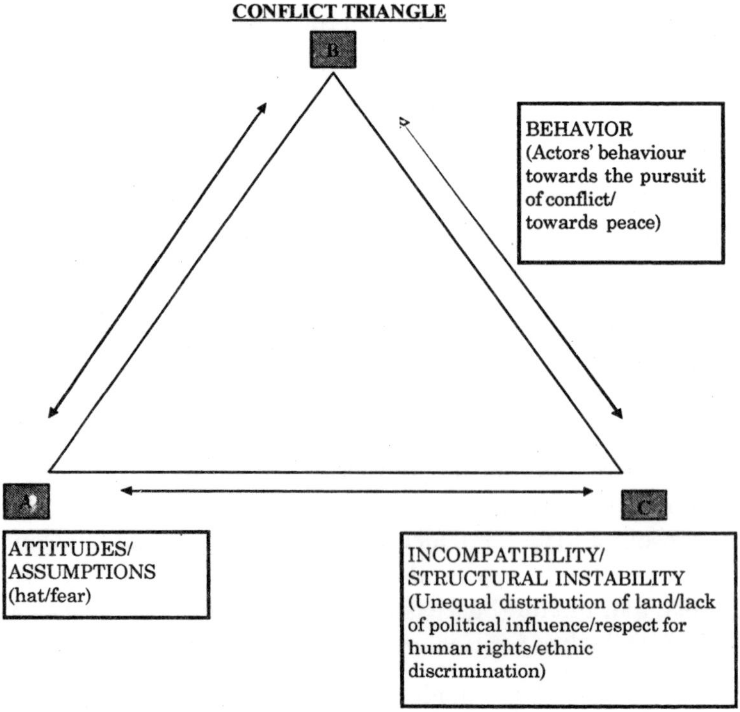

dependent on forest resources; the Adivasis were more reliant on natural resources such firewood as their source of livelihood compared to their Bodo counterparts. But, after the formation of BAC, when the administration of Bodoland came in the hands, the Bodos realized the necessity of forest resources and started protecting it. On the other hand, the Adivasis who were now organizing themselves on the lines of the Bodoland movement continued their reliance on forest recourses because they needed financial support to sustain their movement, which the forest resources could earn for them. This according to Biswajit Daimary furthered the dissatisfaction between the two communities.[16]

Land as a possible cause of Conflict

As the locus of the study is confined to the communities living in the undivided district of Goalpara, it is important to discuss the history of the land relation between the Bodos and the Adivasis.

A brief history of the land relation between the Bodos and the Adivasis of BTAD

To avoid the repetition of 1855-58 Santhal revolt, the British authority disbursed the Santhals to different parts of India. Assam was one such point where the Santhalis were deported in 1859-60.[17] Contrary to popular belief, the Adivasis of the study area were not brought by the Britishers to work in the tea garden (there are some ex-tea garden families who settled down in the area in the later) but were engaged in tilling and various other agricultural activities. In 1862 some Santhalis came to Baokhungi Hajir foothills and after seeking permission from the Bodos started living there.[18]

Members from both Bodo and Adivasi communities were engaged in farming and they used primitive methods of agriculture. To meet their agricultural demands the two communities 'bulldozed' large stretches of forest area and made the same suitable for cultivation.

As mentioned by Idibor Deori, by 1956-66 the Santhals had become a part of the society and were peacefully residing with the Bodos. But gradually a wind of change was brought in by, the establishment of tea gardens followed by influx of immigrant Muslims. These new settlers applied advanced cultivation techniques thus managing an upperhand in agricultural output. Moreover the forest which had for long catered to the requirements of Bodos as well as Santhals was fast shrinking. The resultant of all these changes was increased pressure on land.[19]

Under the stated circumstances the Bodos from Kokrajhar and Gossaigaon area began to look for land elsewhere. And their search for land took them to places like undivided Lakhimpur, Karbi Anglong, Sibasagar, erstwhile North East Frontier Agency (NEFA) and present day Arunachal Pradesh. But unfortunately here too the migrants from Bodoland area had to face the wrath of the local people, as places such as Lakhimpur, Dhemaji and Karbi Anglong were also facing the problem of land scarcity. Here, Deori points at the irresponsible handling of the matter. He alleges that both Government as well as the NGOs failed to deal with the problem properly and did not even try to develop modern agricultural methods and make technically sound practices popular among the peasants. As a result of this, pressure on land and forest mounted, and this gradually strained the relationship between the Bodos and the Santhals.[20]

During the initial years the English East India Company did not pay much attention towards enactment of land and tenure rights in Assam. It was only in 1886 that Assam got its first legal document which provided a legal base to the ryots rights over his land in the form of *'Assam Land and Revenue Regulation,* 1886. Unlike Assam the history of land rights in Goalpara (which was since 1639 a part of Bengal) dates back to 1765 when East India Company acquired the *Dewani of* Bengal. And in 1793, with the introduction of Permanent Settlement 'the tributes/revenues that were to be paid by the territorial chiefs or Rajas of Goalpara were fixed in perpetuity'.[21]

In 1866 the district of Goalpara was merged with Assam but in 1867 Goalpara was placed under the authority of Koch Behar Chief Commissionership. However, in 1874 when Assam became a Chief Commissioner's Province, Goalpara was once again made a part of Assam and it continues to be so even today.

There were 12 permanently settled estates in Goalpara. These "were on the same footing with the Zamindari system of Bengal, introduced by Lord Cornwallis in 1793. The holder of a permanently- settled estate in Goalpara was defined by the Regulation of 1886 as a proprietor with heritary and transferable rights over his holdings, he had the right to transfer his land by sale, mortgage or gift".[22] The then prevailing Zamindari system in Goalpara gave rise to various intermediary land-holders, tenants, sub-tenants and tenant-at-will. The intermediary landholders and the tenants can be classified as:

Jotdars, who held lands directly from the Zamindar at a rate fixed in perpetuity. They sublet their land to cultivators at a higher rate. Hunter observes that the Jotdars "squeezes as much as he can out of the tenants, making over to the landlord the fixed sum which he can out of the tenants, making over to the landlord the fixed sum which he has agreed to pay, and retaining the balance for himself."[23]

Ijaradars, who held land from the Zamindar on fixed rate of rent in perpetuity. While in the case of the Karari peasants the Zamindar made direct settlement with them at a fixed rate of rent, they were tenants - at - will liable to be ejected from their holdings and their rent was subject to augmentation/rise at periodical intervals.

Chukanidars, who held land directly from the Zamindars on contractual basis. The Sakhbas/Khudhbas were those peasants who held land from Zamindar and instead of money rent paid him by providing certain kind of services. Mention may be made of the fact that under the Zamindari estates in Goalpara the peasant actually had no rights on the land they cultivated.

In addition to the mentioned estates there were some temporarily- settled estates that mainly consisted of Eastern Duars (Bijni,Chirang, Sidli, Rupa, and Guma). Except for

Guma the settlements in these Duwars were similar to that of the Ryotwari settlement that prevailed at that time in other districts of Brahmaputra Valley. The important features of Ryotwari System documented by Ramesh Chandra Kalita [24] are as following:

1. The settlement was made directly with the Ryot or peasant with no intermediary agency in between the Government and the Ryots.
2. A right of property of the Ryots in land with hereditary and transferable right was recognized.
3. The rate of assessment agreed upon both by the Ryot and the Government remained invariably fixed and permanent.
4. The land remained in possession of the Ryot so long as he paid the land tax or revenue to the government.
5. Lastly his land was liable to be placed under additional taxation in case improvement was effected through government measures, while the government had no power or authority to enhance the rates of assessment in case improvements were done under individual initiative and effort of the Ryot.

A remarkable change in the land system of Assam was ushered in 1947 with the inclusion of chapter X of the Assam Land & Revenue Regulation 1886. "Under the provision of Chapter X of the Assam Land & Revenue Regulation 1886, 38 belts/blocks covering an area of roughly 15,000 sq. kms and comprising of 2795 villages were constituted by Congress Ministry."[25] Out of 38 belts and blocks 2+1 (part) belts and 1 block covering an area of 723,029 bighas of land falls within the jurisdiction of BTAD area. The main objective behind the creation of these belts/blocks was to check the problem of tribal land alienation. Large part of these belts/blocks were home to a considerable number of non- tribals as well.

Therefore "non- tribals who were permanently living in the proposed belts and blocks on the date of their creation were treated on the same footing as the tribals, with regards to future settlement of wasteland and transfer of patta land." In fact the Assam government on 5th December, 1947 notified the classes of persons who are entitled to protection under Chapter X. The notified classes are 1. Plain Tribals 2. Hill Tribals 3. Tea-Garden Tribals 4. Santhals and 5. Scheduled Castes.[26]

The study of the changing land relations (legal aspects) reveals the fact that unlike many parts of India where discord (relating to land) between communities have their roots in equal land rights here the conflicting parties were not subjected to such kind of discrimination. Perhaps the increasing pressure on the land due to rise in the population of both the communities coupled with other socio-political changes became a cause of brewing tension among the two groups. However, the following observation of Hiren Gohain needs a special mention here: "even when limited autonomy is conceded it turns into a half-measure thanks to insincerity and tampering in fulfilling agreed demand. Ethnic movement and militancy are products of this situation, and their undesirable aspects should not blind us to their genesis in injustice and oppression."[27]

Apart from the secondary sources we also took into account the views of civil society members on the question as to whether the issue of land alienation the reason behind the ethnic turmoil.

Vice president, of Bodo Sahitya Sabha, Taren Boro traces the roots of the Bodos and the Adivasis conflict to the unrestrained migration of the Adivasis people from the various parts of Jharkhand, Chattishgarh and Bihar. This wave of migration added to the already existent Adivasi population but the new settlers could mingle with the old settlers quite easily. The resultant scarcity of revenue and forest land got culminated into the conflict in his opinion. Bodo lamented the fact that many innocent Santhals who had been living since pre-independence period also got killed in the conflict.[28]

According to Dr. Anil Boro from the Department of Folklore, Gauhati University too land became the apple of discord between the communities. His argument stems from the basic argument of land alienation due to the large scale migration into the Bodo heartland and the resulting frustration among the Bodos. He also surmised that there is a possibility of contestations over the ownership of the forest land which got deforested during the Bodo Movement.[29]

Indibor Deori believes that land scarcity is one of the major causes of conflict but not the soul cause. Recollecting the stories narrated to him by his grandfather, Deori informs us that the Adivasis settled in the Gossaigaon area with the due permission of the *gaon bura* or the village headman. At the initial stage majority of the Adivasis worked as laborers in the Bodo households and cultivated fields owned by Bodos, while there were some who tilled their own land. Despite the master servant relation there was co-existence between the two communities.[30]

With the gradual increase in the number of tea gardens in the area, pressure on land began to be felt. But it was not due to the pressure on land exerted by tea gardens that lead to any kind of conflict. It was only towards the last decades of 19th century when migration from East Bengal to this part of India began that pressure on land led to inter-community tension and eventually to inter-community conflict.

However, as already mentioned there is no consensus whether or not land can be regarded as the cause of conflict. The next section deals with those who negate the hypothesis of land as the cause of conflict.

UG Brahma rejecting land alienation as the root of the conflict between the Adivasis and the Bodos, attributed the cause of conflict upon a political conspiracy of an 'outside force'. Brahma instead refers to the recovery of the dead bodies of three Bodo girls, allegedly raped in an Adivasi village. According to him there is not an iota of evidence against any Adivasi men or any Bodo men of being involved in that gruesome act. The whole incident is shrouded in mystery and no inquiry commission has been able to pin up anybody or any community till date. Then he contended that Bodos are not alienated from their land by the Adivasis. So, there is no question of an Adivasi-Bodo conflict on the issue of land.[31]

Sunil Kaul a well known social activist too holds the view that land is not the primary issue of conflict. He referred to multi-ethnic Singapore, a small place that has hardly witnessed any conflict; because of being economically sound. Therefore, he blames economic underdevelopment in the area as the main reason behind the conflict.[32]

Victims' Verdict

As the study progressed, pinpointing the cause(s) of conflict became all the more complex. We therefore decided to take the views of those who were most affected. Through empirical investigation we set to find out the cause of conflict and whether the victims were satisfied with what they have been provided so far. Considering the homogeneous nature of the 'universe' (i.e. the victims), a small sized sample was taken. The samples were collected on a random basis, from among those who were aged between 30- 90 yrs. The reason behind choosing this age group was that people under 30 years were minors when the conflict took place more than a decade ago. A hundred questionnaires were used by two field investigators to gather the required data.

Factors responsible for the conflict were broadly categorized into the following three groups:

(i) Political *(dissatisfaction with the political arrangement, and the territorial boundary of BAC, fear of political marginalization)*

(ii) Socioeconomic *(social inequality and injustice, inter-ethnic distrust and hatred, land alienation)*

(iii) Others *(widespread rumors, killing of three girls, cannot say).*

The following table 1 shows that 58% of the Bodo respondents believed that political factors caused the conflicts. In case of Adivasis, 39% blamed it on socio-political factors. Remarkably a considerable number of respondents from both the communities were not in a position to point out the cause of the conflict.

Table 1: Showing opinion of Bodos and Adivasis on factors responsible for the conflicts

Sl. No	*Factors*	*Bodo %*	*Adivasi %*
1	Political	58	29
2	Socio-economic	22	39
3	Others	20	32
	Total	100	100

More details on the causes of conflict follow.

Political Factor

Among the Bodos who attributed the conflict to political factors, 28% said that *"failure on the part of the state machineries"* contributed the most towards the brewing tension which ultimately led to the violent conflict. A majority (57%) believed that certain core issues were not properly dealt with *"the issue of territorial boundary of BAC"* while, 15% of the respondents believed, *"fear of political marginalization"* was the cause behind the conflict.

In this category, 26% of Adivasis believed that *"fear of political marginalization"* was the cause behind the inter-ethnic clashes. 43% voted for *"the issue pertaining to territorial boundary of BAC"* while 31% said *"failure on the part of the state machineries,"* caused the conflict.

Table 2: Showing opinion of Bodos and Adivasis regarding the political factors responsible for the conflicts

Sl. No	*Factors*	*Bodo %*	*Adivasi %*
1	Failure of the state machineries	28	31
2	Dissatisfied with the territorial boundary of BAC	57	43
3	Fear of political marginalization	15	26
	Total	100	100

Social Factor

Under the "social factors", 15% of the Bodo respondents voted in favour of *"social inequality and injustice"* as the cause of conflict, whereas 60% believed that *"inter-ethnic distrust and hatred"* resulted in the bloodshed. And 25% thought *"problem of land alienation"* to be the cause.

In the case of Adivasis 64% felt *"social inequality and injustice"* was the cause of the conflict while 25% believe a variety of reasons the society registered an unhealthy trend of mutual mistrust making them attribute the cause of the conflict to *"inter-ethnic distrust and hatred"*. And 11% said the cause was *"the problem of land alienation"*.

Table 3: Opinion of Bodos and Adivasis on social factors responsible for the conflicts

Sl. No	*Factors*	*Bodo %*	*Adivasi %*
1	Social inequality and injustice	15	64
2	Inter-ethnic distrust and hatred	60	25
3	The problem of land alienation	25	11
	Total	100	100

Other Factor(s)

In this category, 25% of Bodo respondents ascribed the conflict to *"widespread rumors"*, 46% to *"killing of three girls"*, 29% *"could not"* point out the cause.

On the other hand, 41% Adivasis attributed the causes to *"wide spread rumors"* and 24% to the *"three girls who were believed to have belonged to Bodo community allegedly killed by the Santhals"*, Surprisingly, 35% *could not point out* the cause of the conflict.

Table 4: Showing opinion of Bodos and Adivasis regarding the other factors responsible for the conflicts

Sl. No	*Factors*	*Bodo %*	*Adivasi %*
1	Widespread rumors	25	41
2	Killing of three girls	46	24
3	Cannot say	29	35
	Total	100	100

The above data reveals that land is not the sole cause of the conflict, other factors contributed to the conflict. In addition to the above the respondents were asked if they were satisfied with what has been provided to them so far. None were found to be satisfied. They said they were highly dissatisfied with the poor state of education and health facilities in the relief camps. Moreover, the camp dwellers also complained about the way the government has been dealing with the issue of their rehabilitation.

We traveled to various parts of BTAD including the relief camps to find out the cause of such bitterness. The following chapter reveals our findings.

FOOTNOTES

1. *New International Webster Pocket Dictionary*, new revised edition (2001) India.
2. Jeong, Ho-Won (2008), *Understanding conflict and conflict analysis* Sage Publication Limited, London, pp.5-6.
3. Melander, Erilk, etal, 2004, *How to conduct a conflict analysis* published by Sida.
4. www.conflictsensitivity.org/resource_pack/chapter_2_266.pdf accessed on 2.12.2007.
5. http://www.undp.org/cpr/documents/prevention/integrate/Interagency_framwork_for_conflict_analysis_in_transition_situaton doc accessed on 8.1,2008
6. http://en.wikipedia.org/wiki/Ethnic_conflict accessed on 1.4.2008.
7. Parikh, Sunita (1998) "Religion, Reservation and Riot", in Basu, Amrita, Kohli, Atul (ed), *"Community Conflicts and the state in India"*, Oxford University Press, New Delhi, p.35.
8. Roy, Ramashray, Miri, Sujata, Goswami, Sandhya, (2007) *Northeast India,* Anshaha Publishing House, New Delhi, p.14.
9. XI Lok Sabha Debates, Session I, Monday, May27, 1996/ Jyaistha 6, 1918 (Saka).
10. Interview with Bosco Chermako Chief organizing Secretary Central Committee (AASAA) on 24.4.2008, in Kokrajhar.
11. *Assam Tribune*, May 25, 1996.
12. http://www.undp.org/cpr/documents/prevention/integrate/Interagency_framwork_for_conflict_analysis_in_transition_situations.doc
13. Salomon Gabriel, and Nevo, Baruch eds. (2002), *"Peace Education-The Concept, Principles, and Practices Around the World"* Lawrence Erlbaum Associates, London, p-8.

14. Bhaumik, Subir, *Troubled Periphery: Crisis of India's North East*, P-66, Sage Publication, New Delhi, 2009.

15. Goodhand, Jonathan, (2006), "Aiding Peace", Lynne Rienner Publishers, Inc, USA, pp-11-12.

16. Interview with Biswajit Daimari ,Member of Rajya Sabha, on 25.3.2008 in Dispur, Guwahati.

17 Deowri, Indibor, (2001), *Jangosthi Samasya Atit, Bartaman Bhabisyat,* Journal Emporium, Nalbari.

18. Interview with Indebor Deori on 20.3.2008 in Guwahati.

19. Interview with Indebor Deori on 20.3.2008 in Guwahati.

20. Deowri, Indibor, (2001), *Jangosthi Samasya Atit, Bartaman Bhabisyat,* Journal Emporium, Nalbari.

21. Kalita, Ramesh Chandra, *History of land rights in Brahmaputra Valley*, Ulopi Publications, Tezpur, 1997.

22. *Ibid.* p.26.

23. *Ibid.* p-27.

24. *Ibid.* p.5.

25. Das, J. N. in "Genesis of Tribal Belts and Blocks of Assam" (1986.)in Bordoloi, B.N., "*Alienation of Tribal Land and Indebtedness*, Director, Tribal Research Institute, Asssam, Guwahati, pp.37-38.

26. *Ibid.*

27. Gohain, Hiren, in "Reflection on Ethnicity and Ethnic Movement" in Deka, K.M. & Phukan, K.N.(ed) "*Ethnicity in Assam*", p. 7, Centre for North-East Studies, Dibrugarh, 2001.

28. Interview with Taren Bodo on 1.4.008.

29. Interview with Anil Bodo on 31.3.2008 in Guwahati.

30. Interview with Indebor Deori on 20.3.2008 in Guwahati.

31. Interview with U.G. Brahma, Member of Parliament, Lok Sabha, on 1.4.2008.

32. Interview with Sunil Kaul, social activist, on 2.11.2007.

4

Relief camps: Homes of the destitute

A global change in the character of war was witnessed during 1980s and 1990s, inter-state wars were increasingly been replaced by civil conflicts. This change began to alter the pattern of international refugees. Their number shrunk while of the internally displaced persons or the IDPs increased. Let us begin by knowing the IDPs?

> Persons or group of people who have forced to flee or to leave their homes or places of habitual residence as result of, or in order to avoid, in particular, the effects of armed conflict, situations of generalized violence, violations of human rights or natural or human-made disaster and who have not crossed an internationally recognized border.[1]
>
> Internally displaced people are those forcibly displaced as a result of conflict within their own country. They are distinguished from refugees in that they have not crossed an internationally recognized border as a result of their displacement. [2]

The United Nations Guiding Principles on Internal Displacement defines IDPs:

> Persons or groups of persons who have been forced or obliged to flee or leave their homes or place of habitual residence, in particular as a result of, or in order to, avoid the effects of armed conflict, situation of generalized violence, violation of human rights or natural or human made disasters, and who have not crossed an internationally recognized border.[3]

Since the late 1980s, ethnic conflicts and counter-insurgency operations to oppose movement for greater autonomy have generated thousands of IDPs in India. Assam, the most popular state in Northeast, has not been spared of the problem of IDPs. It has been home to all three categories of IDPs–a) conflict-induced, b) environment-induced, c) man-made or development-induced. Here the discussion is restricted to the first category of IDPs only. Although various types of conflicts in different point of time have caused displacement to massive number of people in the state as well as in this region, statistical data of the exact number of people affected by conflict-induced displacement is absent. Overcoming such impediments, academicians and researchers have shown interest in understanding the problems of these IDPs.

In BTAD the voices of thousands of IDPs who have been languishing in various relief camps for more than a decade now have gone unheard. Neither government agencies nor national/international organizations have shown sustained interest in providing these IDPs with basic human amenities. The young brigade living in the state-run relief camps expressed their bitterness towards the decision makers. Prolonged isolation from the outer world and lack of mission in life have made them idel, in such situations where poverty is rampant and opportunities few and far between the possibility of being lured to anti-social activities increases by manifold.

More than a decade has passed since the conflict took place in May 1996 and May 1998 but a large number of the victims belonging to Adivasi and immigrant community continue to live a life devoid of any access to basic services such as health and education, coupled with continuous state of acute fear and uncertainty about future. Though the relief camp inmates have been living in sub-human conditions in BTAD for more than 10 years now, local organizations and state and central government have not taken proper steps to alleviate their problems. Organizations such as the Lutherian World Service (LWS) and ANT (Action Northeast Trust) have been exception with their humanitarian missions. The problems of these IDPs have over the years become so complex that 'periodic' interventions made by NGOs are not enough to bring in a sustainable solution to the problem.

As has already been mentioned the area has fallen victim of ethnic conflicts at different point in time, starting with the clash between Bodos and Koch-Rajbonshis in 1989, between Bodos and immigrant Muslims in 1993, Bodo and Adivasis in 1996 and 1998 and Bodos and Muslims in October 2008. These conflicts have left lakhs of people homeless. Taking advantage of short lived public memory (read public pressure) both the state as well as the central government have so far succeeded to neglect the plight of these dwellers. Though some legislators like Wazed Ali Chowdhury, Ardhendu Kumar Dey, Abu Saleh Najmuddin and Silviews Kondopan, took up various issues relating to the ethnic conflict as well as rehabilitation of these IDPs in the state legislative assembly. Substantive steps did not followed these discussions. Ten years down the line, the issues of the IDPs remain unattended to. Additionally, mainstream media failed to project the seriousness of their problem, like many other problems of the Northeastern region. In most cases NE finds space in national media only when large scale bombing and casualties are caused by insurgent or terrorists in the area. As a result, "this narrow focus has encouraged the widespread perception that all problems in the NE region are due to insurgency. This effectively masks the underlying structural problems of poor governance, unemployment and lack of investment in the social sector, which, as elsewhere in the region, are significant causes of conflict."[4]

According to, "Action Plan for Rehabilitation of the Refugees, 1993, 1996 and 1998 Ethnic Violence" Kokrajhar (1998), in May 1996 a total of 42,214 families consisting of 202,684 persons were rendered homeless. These displaced were sheltered in 61 relief camps. The report further states that the resumption of the conflict in May 1998 added to the number of displacees. Out of 48,556 families consisting of 314,342 persons who were displaced from their native places, of 34,348 families consisting of 219,108 inmates were sheltered in 63 relief camps in Kokrajhar and Gosssaigaon area.

Presently the number of relief camps in the BTAD stands at 33. The total population of the relief camps as per government records is 71,630.

The camp listed in table 5 and 6 were visited since August 2007.

Table 5: Relief camps visited during August 2007 to June 2009

Sl. No.	*Names of the Relief Camps*	*District / Circle*
1	Joypur	Kokrajhar revenue circle
2	Bishmuri	Kokrajhar revenue circle
3	Veterinary Complex, Bengtol	Sidli – Chirang revenue circle
4	Joypur (A)	Kokrajhar
5	Joypur (B)	Kokrajhar
6	Bishmuri (B)	Kokrajhar
7	Runikhata & Bhurpar	Sidli-Chirang
8	Serfunguri (SATC)	Gossaigaon
9	Hazarkia	Gossaigaon
10	Golajhar	Gossaigaon
11	Bhumka-Maligaon	Gossaigaon
12	Santipur	Gossaigaon
13	Kachugaon	Gossaigaon (Encroacher)
14	Sapkata	Gossaigaon (Encroacher)
15	No. 3 Phulkumari (Vidyapur)	Bongaigaon
16	Alengibazar	Kokrajhar
17	Anthiabari – Tinali	Kokrajhar
18	Bangaldoba relief camp	

Table 6: Showing partly rehabilitated relief camps

Sl. No.	*Partly Rehabilitated Camps*	*District / Circle*
1.	Patgaon(Adivashi)	Gossaigaon
2.	Deosri(B)	Sidli-Chirang
3.	Alengibazar	Gossaigaon
4.	Dhanpur(Karigaon)	Kokrajhar
5.	Athiabari-Tiniali	Gossaigaon
6.	Simbergaon	Kokrajhar

It was observed that the conflict that caused displacement had some direct effect on education, nutrition and health of the children, youth and women. The following section will deal at length with the many difficulties faced by children, youth and women living in the camps.

1.1 Education

Backdrop

Prior to the conflicts too the education scenario was not satisfactory. Nevertheless, villages in the area had access to at least primary and at many places secondary schools. But the functioning of the existing schools began to be hampered as the Bodo movement changed and resorted to violence and *bandhs* (closure of schools, colleges, offices and business establishments) for achieving its goal. Owing to frequent *bandhs* in the area educational institutes were unable to cover their syllabi on time. This backlog became an obstacle for many who desired to pursue their studies outside the then Bodoland or the state. Soon after the inter-ethnic clashes there was further deterioration in the overall educational scenario of the area. Evidence confirms that ethnic conflicts in BTAD adversely effected the education of children belonging to both Bodo as well as non- Bodo communities.[5]

The following section accounts for the challenges, which some of the conflict-induced IDPs continue to face even today.

One of the immediate effects of conflict on the children is disruption/discontinuation of schooling. Out of more than 27 million children estimated to lack access to education in emergency situations, significant number is internally displaced.[6] For these children not only is their educational development denied but they are deprived of other important benefits as well. Here, too the situation is not different. Soon after the conflict erupted, schools were closed down not for security reasons but also because they were been used as shelters by those affected by conflict.

A sizeable number of young boys and girls living in the relief camps were school goers when the unfortunate incident took place. The conflict followed by displacement did not give them any chance of resuming their studies. However, Runikatha - Bhurpar camp is among few camps which have access to government school. The school is a stone's throw from the camp but the children of the camp are unable to avail the benefits of education. Children who were in standard II and III were not in a position to recognize alphabets. Explaining why children could not recognize the alphabets, Dara Kisko an elderly camp inmate said,

> "They cannot learn anything, their teacher speaks in Assamese and they do not understand Assamese. We can speak in Assamese because we had Assamese friends and neighbors. But these children grew up speaking only their mother tongue. They just go to school for the sake of it."

Since the children from this Adivasi camp do not know any other language, other than their own they fail to comprehend the medium (Assamese) of instruction and the language of their teachers who speak in Assamese. Hence, they lack interest in their lessons and most of them end up learning nothing. Though Principle 23 of the UN Guiding Principles on Internal Displacements has affirmed the right of the IDPs to receive an education respectful of their culture, language and identity, policy makers are yet to show any interest in this regards. In a multilingual society like that of Northeast India lot of planning is necessary for providing minimum education to the children.

The position of girl child and her accessibility to education needs a special mention here. During the conflict as well as

in the post-conflict situations girls not only lose their freedom of mobility; they also have to compromise on certain other spheres of life. Education is a sacrifice expected from and made mostly by the female child of the family. Bimla Murmur of Runikatha-Bhurpar camp is one such case. In spite of the easy accessibility of education, Bimla is not in position to avail it. When asked why Bimla, she said:

> "How will I go to school? my mother has gone out to work and I have to look after my siblings and my ailing grandmother. My father died few years back. He died of dysentery."

However, in some of the relief camps like Kasugaon the education scenario is not as deplorable, thanks to the initiatives taken by Lutheran World Service (LWS). Rupa Tiru's success is a testimony of healthier education environment that prevails in Kasugaon camp. A standard X student, Rupa harbors a positive attitude towards life. She told us:

> "I know there are many problems in our lives but I think if I study well things will change for better, Even our teachers say so."

When she was asked about her aim in life she promptly replied that she wanted to be a teacher. Braving the daily hazards of camp life Rupa attends her classes regularly and she was found to have command over the subjects taught to her. English been her favorite subject she unhesitantly recited some lines from Robert Frost's poem, "Stopping by the Woods on a Snowy Evening"

> "The woods are lovely, dark and deep,
>
> But I have promises to keep.
>
> And miles to go before I sleep."

However, the school service provided by LWS ended in 2007.

Not only the girl child, the wrath of the conflict and the absence of post-conflict institutional support has affected the lives of thousands of young children who were born in the relief camps. According to UNICEF report on the *"The State of the World's Children 2001"*, the period from birth to 3 years age is a very crucial period in a child's life. It further says that this period "influences how the rest of childhood and adolescence unfolds".[7] However, this important phase is often neglected by policymakers in this part of the world.

Golajar relief camp in Gossaigaon has a population of 4,173. Out of this the population of minors stands at 1,700. Most of the children in the camp aged between 2.5-8 yrs were playing with piglets and chicks. Kunti Besra an old lady and grand mother of two of the children playing said:

"These piglets need supervision and our children need recreation, so I allow my grandsons to play with them. Otherwise in this place they have nothing else to do."

Play and leisure have been acknowledged by educationist all over the world as an essential part as a child's life. Article 31 of the Convention on the Rights of the Children (CRC), ratified by India has also underscored the importance of recreation to children. However, the IDP children in Golajar and other relief camps have so far been denied proper leisure and play activities, and it is due to absences of these facilities they are left with no choice but to play with piglets, chicks, etc. And, in the absence of any educational package that could have helped these IDP school dropouts resume their studies because of lack of skill enhancement opportunity the number of frustrated, unskilled youth has reached an alarming level. The level of dissatisfaction among the young brigade is evident from what an inmate of veterinary. Complex Bangtol camp, high school dropout Sibu Besra (20) said:

> "How can anyone think of going to school in such a situation? We could not come out of the horror of conflict, and attend schools. And after so many years I don't want to study any more. Our lives will continue to be as it is. No one ever did anything and they will never do anything for us."

This is not the voice of Sibu alone; his frustrations are echoed by his counterparts living in similar situation elsewhere in BTAD. Dhiru Madri from Runikatha -Bhurbar camp echoes Sibu sentiment. Madri says:

> "I was in class 6 when the conflict took place. I was the brightest of my six siblings. My family had high expectations from me. But today everything has changed, I could not complete my studies, tell me who can study when there is constant fear and uncertainty. I could not fulfill the expectations of my family. I have no work here so I and my friends loiter around the whole day."

Madri further says:

> "I want to learn driving, so that I can go to town and work. But here we do not have any driving school, and the fees in town is so high how will I learn to drive?"

Besides the ray of hope which was more than evident in the bright eyes of young Rupa, the overall education scenario in the camps in BTAD area wears a gloomy look.

The conflict in BTAD area threw open, the floodgates of challenges to the society in general and more particularly to women besides the children. Sexual assault and exploitation, unwanted pregnancies are some of the gender violence experienced by women during wartimes, sexual violence has reached epidemic proportions, for instance up to 500,000 women were raped, many at gunpoint, in Rwanda alone in 1994.[8] And contrary to genuine believe gender violence does not ebb with the end of fighting, post-conflict situations are worse. Interestingly, though conflict inflict untold miseries, suffering and pain, besides gender related violence on women, in some cases conflicts empower women socially, politically and economically.[9] This mostly happens in such conflict situations where there is high mortality rate of men and/or migration of male population. However, as and when fighting ends and male population returns the empowerment gained by women in the absence of male counterpart begins to erode. It can therefore, be argued that though conflict in some cases bring positive shift in gender-roles and in some cases it even improves women rights unfortunately, such kind of opportunities rarely sustain when normalcy returns. And with the return of normalcy women are compelled to retire from their war time responsibilities and resume their 'natural' duties as care givers, home makers etc. More importantly conflicts which give women an opportunity to unlock the doors to empowerment are few and far between; in most cases impact of conflict on women is devastatingly negative.

Women caught in the BTAD conflicts bore the brunt of negative impact of conflict in the form of gender violence and exploitation. But they were not fortunate enough to embark upon political or economic empowerment. Why the women folk could not make the most out of conflict is a debatable issue. One may argue that the low intensity conflicts of 1996-98 in the area did not claim as many male lives or forced migration of as many males as was required to create a vacuum that would have given the women folk of the area an opportunity for empowerment. Apart from situational constraints what else made the lives of tens of thousands of women's lives miserable? It is here that the role of the state towards safeguarding the weaker section (here women), which finds expression in the constitution of the country (right to equality) as well, needs to be closely examined. The United Nations Guiding Principles on Internal Displacement, Principle 4 states that minors, expectant mothers, mothers with young children, and female heads of families, among others are people who need special care. Apart from the UN Guiding Principle the 1979 Convention on the Elimination of All Forms of Discrimination against Women (CEDAW) and the 1999 Optional Protocol sets out specific steps for states to become proactive in their efforts to eliminate discrimination against displaced women. CEDAW Article 2 states that public authorities, individuals, organizations and enterprises should refrain from discrimination against women, similarly, Article

3 reiterated women's right to get protection from sexual harassment.[10] Unfortunately, the relief assistances provided by the state hardly show any signs of gender sensitivity. Some of the narrations in the following section give an insight into the hardships which the women folk faced during the conflict and it continues to haunt them even to these days.

1.2 Health and sanitation

The boons of popular health schemes like National Rural Health Mission (NRHM) are yet to reach the relief camp dwellers. Most of the camp dwellers do not have access to health care centers. However, Veterinary Complex Bangtol relief camp, which shelters 528 inmates, is an exception. The health center of the area is situated just opposite to Bangtol Veterinary Complex relief camp. But surprisingly the camp dwellers prefer quacks to doctors and indigenous herbs to medicine. According to Damu Besra the president of the relief camp,

> "When anyone in the camp falls sick, they do not go to the health centre, because there is no medicine. So, the inmates prefer to be at home rather than going to the health centre. The health centre staffs advise us to buy medicines from market. Tell me what is the use of going there?"

Moreover, the nutrition level of the inmates is another area which needs a thorough study. Presently the camp inmates are entitled to ration for only 10 days in a month. The ration consists of only rice. There is no especial consideration for pregnant women or growing children. Biru Hasda from the same camp complains:

> "In a month we get ration for 10 days only. An adult gets 600gms and children get 400gms of rice. We don't have any means of livelihood here. Some inmates catch fish from the nearby lakes, pond etc. Some work in small business establishments. This is how we have been surviving all these years. No one thinks for us. When you return to the city please tell someone to help us."

If that were not enough, pregnant and lactating mothers did not receive adequate attention and care in the relief camps, during the months immediately after conflict. Sukumari Hasda ex-secretary of *Adivasi Mahila Samity* (AMS) speaks about the hazards that she and her colleagues had to take while lobbying for baby food for the newborns in the relief camps. She said:

> "Expecting mothers ate nothing for days, so you can imagine the condition of babies born out of hungry mothers. These women were not in a position to feed their new-born. As a woman I could understand the condition of the mothers. So, our samity decided to do something for the newborns. Some of us even went to Dispur (state capital) so that the babies have something to eat. The situation was so tensed but keeping aside all our fear we visited the administration, and ultimately baby foods were supplied to camp inmates."

Complications during pregnancy, childbirth, claimed many lives immediately after the conflict and unfortunately such death continues even today in many of the relief camps. Narration from an eye witness of one such incident follows. Tikhri of Vet. Complex Bangtol camp said:

> "Immediately after the conflict, many women gave birth to children in the open, without any medical attention or help from mid-wives. I myself have seen a lady wailing during her labour pain, but there was no one to help her and she ultimately died. I will never forget this incident in my lifetime."

Decades have passed but little has changed as childbirth continues to take place in the dingy, unhygienic dwellings of the inmates. Vet Complex Bangtol is not an exception; the other camps are no better. However, the reason varies. For Bangtol camp inmates the nearby health center does not have adequate facilities to assist during childbirth. According to Bismuri camp inmates the health machineries are situated too far to be accessed by a woman undergoing labour pain. This is what Sundari Tiru had to say:

> "Doctors have never visited us. A signboard reads nearest health centre Patgaon, but we don't go there, it is too far for us. Even male inmates who fall sick cannot go to Patgaon. How can a pregnant woman go? When we fall sick we visit pharmacists in Bismuri area. And there are dhai maas' (midwives) to assist us during childbirth."

At many other camps like Hazarkia, Golajhar, Bhumka-Maligaon the inmates were found to be unaware of Jannani Suraksha Yojana under NRHM which aims to reduce the Maternal Mortality Ratio (MMR) and Infant Mortality Rate (IMR) and to increase the number of institutional deliveries by providing incentives to the mother.

World Health Organisation (WHO) defines health as, a state of complete physical, mental and social well-being and not merely the absence of disease or infirmity.[11] Mental wellness refers to a positive attribute, such that a person can reach enhanced levels of mental health, even if they do not have any diagnosable mental health condition. This definition of mental health highlights emotional well-being, the capacity to live a full and creative life, and the flexibility to deal with life's inevitable challenges.[12]

Going by the above definitions the inter-ethnic conflicts not only affected the victims physically, it also posed serious threat to victims' mental health. Direct exposure to violence may result in acute psychological disorder. Conflict victims are vulnerable to some of these long term psychological effects like lack of concentration, depression, anxiety etc. we came across such cases of conflict related psychological problems. Surprisingly it was found that there is no provision to help victims of conflict who were battling to come out of conflict related shocks. Absences of trauma healing centers have left the likes of Tuli Besra, alone to cope with their fears, shocks and anxieties. Tuli, 80, is an inmate of Bismuri relief camp. She was found to be too shocked to narrate her pains. Her son Mangal Murmu narrated the reason behind his mother's silence –

> "Don't ask her anything she will not reply. She has stopped talking since that fateful day, when 29 members of our extended family were killed. She was witness to some of the horrific killings. And since then she hardly talks."

The difficulties faced by these camp dwellers are many, the problems faced by women and young girls have a different dimension which often goes unaddressed. In the initial days the relief camps did not provide for the much needed private space for the female inmates. Female inmates above had to compromise on such bare necessities as maintenance of hygiene. Kamli Tiru (name changed) from Kasugaon relief camp where the number of female inmates is 1,898, shares with us the kind of adjustments she and other females of the camp made during their menstruation period:

> "We ran out of our homes without carrying anything. I could not find anything in the relief material which could help me to maintain minimum hygiene during those days, not even a piece of cloth. With no other option I started looking for some sort of isolation where I could sit the whole day. Others also did the same. Please, don't remind me of those horrible days."

More then 10 years down the lane females in the camps continue to be devoid of their 'space'. The study found that there were no provisions of latrines for the inmates of the camps. Even today they continue to attend to nature's call in the open or near the banks of rivers or streams. Simri Tudu from Bhumka-Maligaon says:

> "During the day time we manage to go to the nearby woods. But at night we cannot go too far. So, at night we look for isolation and sit wherever possible."

However, there are few fortunate families who with the help and assistance from the government officials could return to their original villages, Bishnu Murmu's family is one. Bishnu today has his own house to live but surprisingly most of them like to spend their time in the relief camps. Because though they have left the relief camps for their native villages (which have considerable number of Bodo families) they are still unable to bid farewell to their fears and mistrust. Sibbu Munda has a different complain:

> I got back my house but what will I eat? Here (relief camp) at least my family got some food to eat, but in my own village I cannot till my own land. Bodos and we (Advasis) planted jackfruit saplings together, but the fruits are enjoyed by Bodos alone, as we cannot go back to our farms...

Interrupting Sibbu, Barka Hembrem the president of Kasugaon relief camp said that the district administration have refused to accept their demand of a revised list of camp dwellers (CDs). As a result ration entitled for the CDs is not in proportion with the population of the relief camps. In addition to this the CDs have to contend with corrupt practices to get their monthly dues. In Barkha's words:

> From godown keeper to officer-in-charge, we pay bribe (it ranges from Rs.50-100) to everyone. In addition, each time the truck loaded with our ration passes by certain points like the dadagiri hotel, Goruphela LP School near Kasugaon Police Station goons demand donation from the truck drivers. We reimburse the truck driver.

Some of the queries which hounded us got answered as we traveled from one camp to another. The president of Veterinary Bangtol camp pointed at various problems that the CDs faced but almost lost his control when we tried to know about his relationship with his political representative, to which he replied:

> We will come out with dao if anyone comes asking for votes this time. Politicians have been using us for so many years now. They only promise of rehabilitating us, but they have not fulfilled their promise.

We sympathized with them but we were not able to estimate their level of frustration. It was only after several visits that we ultimately realized that on our first visit we had underestimated the pangs of the CDs. Perhaps any third party will need as much time as we took or a little more to get a correct estimation of their problems. But 10 years is too long time for the state administrative machinery to assuage their problem.

Overview of Koch-Rajbonshi and Immigrant Muslim Relief Camps

In addition to Adivasi relief camps we also visited the relief camps resided by Koch Rajbonshi and immigrant Muslims.

It was in 1989 that the first conflict running on the ethnic lines took place in present day BTAD, in this Bodos and Koch Rajajbonshis confronted with each other. Two decades after the unfortunate incident took place about 643 families which were affected in the conflict are yet to get their rightful compensation. Immediately after the conflict they had to flee their villages and take shelter in temporary relief camps provided by the state government in school buildings in Bongaigaon, Chapaguri, Dhaligaon etc. After spending months in such shelters which lacked basic human amenities like provision for sanitation, facility for proper drinking water and adequate medical aid. Many inmates of the relief camp succumbed to diseases like jaundice, diarrhea and viral fever.

Hirala, leader of number 1 Phulkumari relief camp laments the fact that due to the then prevailing situation even the last rites of the deceased could not to be performed properly. In 1990 a rehabilitation package which consisted of ½ bighas of land and cash compensation of Rs. 2,500 was given to each family. Today these displaced persons live in Vidyapur area which is situated 40 km from Bongaigaon. There are three such settlements in Vidyapur viz. number 1 Phulkumari, number 2 Phulkumari and number 2 Bamunitilla *Sarnarthi Sibir* (relief camp).However, settlers of this land were not provided legal land deeds (*miyadi patta*). The inmates of these camps complain that Rs. 2500 was an inadequate amount to meet their various needs. In the absence of agricultural land they had to depend on other source of income like wage labour, collection of wood from the nearby forest, fishing, making various products with bamboo etc. Thanks to the farsightedness of some inmates who realized the necessity of education for their children and its future impact on their lives, accordingly they put forward their demand for the same. But, their demands were turned down by state authorities by citing the excuse of non-availability of land.

This did not stagger the determination of the inmates and each family decided to donate a part of their land for the construction of school. And with due permission from the administration, 3 no. Phulkumari Sarnarthi Sibir, Lower Primary school saw the light of the day in December 1990. It had a modest beginning with a makeshift structure, two teachers Sapan Kumar Nath and Parmeshwar Nath and about 50 students. Almost two decades after the establishment of the school the inmates feel that the school has made a great contribution in their live. Gautam Rai one of the inmates who is employed as a sales person (in a shopping mall in Pune) feels,

> Our school taught us many things. Besides helping us to remain optimistic in life, and for whatever I have achieved in life, I am thankful to God and my school.

Hiralal Rai, one of the leaders of the camp inmates informs:

> Many youths from the camps are employed in cities like Pune, Bangaluru, Guwahati, Delhi etc. this trend has led to economic well being of the inmates in comparison to other non-Bodos who fell victim of ethnic conflict. Without education this would not have been possible.

Most of the camp dwellers earn their livelihood by working in the construction sites in cities like Guwahati, Pune, Mumbai, etc. Others go to hills (salmara, nagkata) to collect firewood which they sell, to sustain themselves and their families.

However, the elderly members of these relief camps consider themselves to be fortunate compared to those who are still toiling in various relief camps in BTAD, because

> We at least have a piece of land to call our own, our children and grand children got the opportunity to study and as the area is well connected with the Bongaigaon town we could opt for daily wage, which helped us to sustain ourselves during those hard time us to forget many of our pains.

Unfortunately the younger lot, does not agree with their elders, their grievances are deep rooted and in most cases Rajbonshi youths complain:

> Since our grandfathers did not take up arms and rather succumbed to the whims of the Bodos we are left with limited options today. But if government continues to neglect the demand of our community in future as well (referring to the demand for Kammatapur)[13]we will not repeat the past mistake and if necessary will take up arms.

Small crowd of young boys and girls who had gathered around us nodded in unison to the above comment made by Madhav Rajbonshi (name changed).

The relief camp resided by immigrant Muslims are no different than those of Adivasis. We visited the Bangaldoba relief camp which is today home to 4,957 displaced persons. And as we stepped down from our vehicle naked and semi-naked children ran towards us, they were expecting eatables or at least toffees, but we had strict instructions from our local resource persons that we should not carry any food item for distribution.

As expected children were disappointed as they discovered we had nothing to offer them. Soon were surrounded by about 100 men belonging to different age group, they were all waiting for their chance to speak out their problems. After some primary queries like how long they have been homeless, to which they said that since 1993 they have been staying in relief camps, they also narrated their problems which were similar to the problems faced by the Adivasi CDs. However, unlike the Adivasi CDs most of them were no longer looking for work in BTAD. Instead they go to Bhutan and work as daily labourers, carpenters, masons etc. Zahkir Ali told us:

> We earn handful there (Bhutan), people are also good, what else can we ask for?

In Bhutan they earn between Bhutanes Nugultrum 100-150. More importantly, back in India they need not go through the hassles of currency exchange as Nugultrum is accepted in most parts of BTAD. This means that they can work freely in Bhutan and their families can spend the amount in BTAD. Tomsher Ali another elderly from the relief camp says

> We prefer to work in foreign land (Bhutan) than to remain confined to the camp areas, living a helpless life, in our own land.

Tomsher *shahib* (as addressed by the camp inmates) was referring the period just after the conflict between the Bodos and the immigrant Muslims, when the later had to remain within the limited relief camp area, or else they were threatened to be killed. Tomsher *shahib* further says:

> I will die after few years, but my grandchildren and other children of the camp have a long way to go. When I think of their future I cannot sleep properly. The camp is yet to have a school; children cover several kilometers, to reach school. Everything is so uncertain......

Both men and women were living in this relief camps were well aware of our visit, and hence, whenever we photographed their children they cautioned them not to smile as this would give the world a wrong message. In one such instance Razia Begum was heard of saying:

> Don't show your teeth, as if you have all the happiness of whole world. If you pose to be happy now, remember we will remain sad forever.

Unlike the Adivasi women, women of Bangaldoba relief camp remain confined in the four walls of there dingy dwellings. Though the men folk from the camp argued that it was mostly due to security reasons that the women folk preferred indoors, however, they could not substantiate their claims when we asked as to why the relief camp women did not attend informal meeting with us, they kept silent.

However, when we insisted to meet the women folk they readily agreed to guide into their dwellings. Most of the women we meet were busy with household chores. There were few (mostly elderly women of the family) who was seen working in kitchen gardens.

Though, these camp dwellers survived the inter-ethnic clashes. But their struggle for life continues to these days. Their biggest enemy today is – hunger, unemployment, and lingering fear of an unsecured future. All these are greatly responsible for distancing sustainable peace from the area.

FOOTNOTES

1. Smelser, Neil J & Baltes, Paul B, *International Encyclopedia of the Social & Behavioural Sciences*, Vol. 19 p.12898.

2. *Out of the margins:* Securing a voice for internally displaced people: lessons from Georgia cited in http://www.cr.org/ ourwork/caucasus/ documents/Georgia_securing_a_voice_for_IDPs_ report_ lowres_ web.pdf accessed on 23.1.2010.

3. United Nations Guiding Principles on Internal Displacement, An Assamese translation with the original English Text included (translated by Baruah, Sanjib, Das, Arup Jyoti & Lahkar, Abinash, Centre for Northeast India, South and Southeast Asia Studies, OKDISCD, Guwahati.

4. Children Affected by Armed Conflict in South Asia: A review of trends and issues identified through secondary research (January 2002), RCS Working Paper No.7, Refugee Study Centre.

5. Bhan, Suslheela (1999), *Impact of Ethnic Violence on Youth,* Shipra Publications, New Delhi, pp.138-139.

6. Women's Commission for Refugee Women and Children, *Global Survey on Education in Emergencies* (February 2004), p. iii and p. 9.

7. Early Childhood cited at http://www.unicef.org/sowc01/ accessed on 25.8.2008.

8. Women and Armed Conflict cited in http://www.iansa.org/women/ documents/women_armed_conflict.pdf accessed on 20.5.2009.

9. Manchanda, Rita (2001), Ambivalent Gains in South Asian Conflicts, in Meintjes, Sheila etal. (eds) *The Aftermath: Women in Post-Conflict Transformation,* Zed Books, London, p.99.

10. United Nations Guiding Principles on Internal Displacement (translated by Baruah, Sanjib, Das,Arup Jyoti & Lahkar, Abinash) Centre for Northeast India, South and Southeast Asia Studies, OKDISCD, Guwahati.

11. Preamble to the Constitution of the World Health Organization as adopted by the International Health Conference, New York, 19-22 June, 1946; signed on 22 July 1946 by the representatives of 61 States (Official Records of the World Health Organization, no. 2, p. 100) and entered into force on 7 April 1948.

12. http://en.wikipedia.org/wiki/Mental_health.

13. Das, Arup Jyoti (2009), *Kamatapur and the Koch Rajbanshi Imagination.*

5

Scars of Conflict: On livelihood and other social spheres

> *"Bodos and we (Advasis) planted jackfruit saplings together, but the fruits are enjoyed by Bodos alone, as we cannot go back to our farms".* Sibbu Munda

Many camp dwellers Sibbu. Their complains often find expression in the form of echo petty feud between the two groups (Bodos and Adivasis), especially in local markets, isolated paddy fields and deserted streets. Past injustice, real or perceived, if not addressed with care is bound to create tensions in the future. To stop the navigation of negative emotions amongst members of the groups involved in conflict at some point in time it is important that they realize the need for some kind of communication which may ideally take the shape of a dialogue so that their past experiences do not become the cause of new conflicts. Such a process is dubbed as reconciliation. The word reconciliation is derived from the Latin word *conciliatus,* which means "coming together". In simpler terms "Reconciliation= Closure + healing: closure in the sense of not reopening hostilities, healing in the sense of been rehabilitated".[1]

Though we know what reconciliation is, the route to its success is yet to be known. The reconciliation process has several stages and involves the use of various tools ranging from healing, truth-telling, restorative justice and reparations. Reconciliation is that process "by which parties that have experienced an oppressive relationship or a destructive conflict with each other move to attain or to restore a relationship that they believe to be minimally acceptable."[2] It is a way of advancing peace and, optimally, justice as well. The proximity of newer conflicts increases by manifold in cases where the agonies and injustice of past conflict(s) has not received the deserving attention or/and the conflict(s) overtly tilted the balance of power in favour of one of the conflicting groups. In such cases the need and importance of reconciliation mechanism becomes all the more important. Unfortunately, despite the reoccurrence of violent conflicts in various points in time in BTAD reconciliation has never been considered seriously.

To confirm the 'negative' changes in the sphere of social interaction (which includes social as well as economic relationship) and such other effects of the inter-ethnic conflict in the study area, we resorted to empirical investigation. Considering the homogeneous nature of the 'universe' (comprising of conflict victims) as well as the time limit, a small sample was taken. The samples were collected on a random basis.

Rural India invariably views with suspicion strangers do make complex questions about their lives sound simpler. It was no different in our case taking us 23 weeks and many visits to earn the confidence of the respondents. We were careful in making the relief camp inmates comfortable as they answeed our queries. Besides been hesitant and unwilling to answer, the respondents were more interested to know if we belonged to any political party before opening up. We did not give up even after been treated rudely, and in some cases threatened. The rudeness we realized, reflected the frustration and anger among the inmates. They had every right to feel aggrieved after being largely ignored for more than a decade.

Luckily, our *modus operandi* of first winning the confidence of the relief camp president (every relief camp has a president chosen by consensus among the inmates) and then talking to individuals paid off. We came across a few who were forthcoming with their views on issues that concerned them. However, most of them preferred to answer in either yes or no. The experience was unforgettable, we negotiated waves of biases, half-truth and subjective explanations, encountered with some men and women who displayed great sense of objectivity in answering our queries and sharing with us tales of tolerance and trust displayed by members of other community due to which they today live to tell us their stories.

For assessing the change in the social-economic relationship between the Bodos and Adivasis, we used four indicators of social interaction. They are:

(i) Participation in intercommunity festivals

(ii) Peer group

(iii) Professional relationship

(iv) Means of livelihood.

Participation in inter-community festivals

It was found that prior to the conflict 68% of Bodos and 88% of Adivasis took part in almost all types of inter-community festivals that included religious festivals as well as social functions (marriages, rites performed during birth and death, etc). However, after the conflict only 15% Bodos and 12% Adivasis said that they participate in each others festivals.

Table 7: Level of participation in inter-community festivals before and after conflict

Before		*Communities*	
		Bodo %	*Adivasis %*
Participation in inter-community festivals	Yes	68	88
	No	32	12
Total		100	100
After		*Bodo%*	*Adivasi %*
Participation in inter-community festivals	Yes	15	12
	No	85	88
Total		100	100

Reasoning the decrease in their participation, Bodo respondents said that prior to the conflict they had Adivasis as their neighbors and took part in their festivals. But conflicts at various phases altered the demography of the villages and the number of inter-community villages declined. While most Bodos continue to live in the native villages they inhabited before the conflict, majority of the Adivasis moved to relief camps or in villages where their community has a strong presence. As a result participating in each others festivals is no more a social obligation, the Adivasi are not happy about it and at the same time are not ready to entertain guests, at least those they perceive to have caused them miseries.

For the Adivasi respondents taking part in the social festivals of the Bodo was a social as well as obligation, as many of them worked in the fields of Bodos and also lent a helping hand for domestic chores or worked as domestic help at Bodo households. Unfortunately, this is no longer the case.

Some of the Adivasi respondents complained that, immediately after the conflict they had to confine themselves within the relief camp, this had a "paralyzing effect on their already shattered lives."[3] Under such circumstances the question of taking part in 'others' hardly arises. The tendency of the Bodos and Adivasis to refer to each other as the 'other' indicate the existence of unease between the two communities.

Peer group

In our attempt to assess the state of inter-community friendship, the randomly selected respondents were asked to name two of their closest friends before the conflict and after the conflict. 70% and 84% of the total respondents from the Bodo and Adivasi community respectively did not seem to give much importance to ethnic affiliation while choosing their friends prior to the conflict. But post-conflict, 80% Bodos and 97% Adivasis said that ethnic affiliation mattered. Though some of the Bodo respondents insisted that still try to maintain the same relation with the Adivasis, the latter said they no longer have faith in the Bodos. The following table reflects the above stated findings.

Table 8: Showing inter-community peer relationship before and after conflict

Before		*Communities*	
		Bodo %	*Adivasis %*
Peers belonging to other community	Yes No	70 30	84 16
Total		100	100
After		*Bodo%*	*Adivasi %*
Peers belonging to other community	Yes No	20 80	3 97
Total		100	100

Professional relationship

The two communities involved in the inter-ethnic clashes

shared professional relation since the time they have been co-habiting in the area. Such professional relations were mostly related to the field of agriculture, where Adivasis, in most cases tilled agricultural land owned by the Bodos.

We tried to assess the kind of professional relation that the two communities shared before and after the conflict. Accordingly the respondents were asked about the kind of professional relationship that they shared from other community before and after the conflict.

Table 9 indicates a healthy trend in the professional relationship between respondents of both the communities before conflict. However, the same table reflects a change in the inter-community professional relationship after the conflict. It shows that there has been a drastic fall in the percentage of individuals sharing professional relationship with members from 'other' ethnic group.

Table 9: Showing inter-community professional relationship before and after conflict

Before		*Communities*	
		Bodo %	*Adivasis %*
Professional Relationship with other community	Yes No	82 18	86 14
Total		100	100
After		*Bodo%*	*Adivasi %*
Professional Relationship with other community	Yes No	45 55	25 75
Total		100	100

The following section gives a detailed picture of the changes in the professional relationship between the two communities after the ethnic upheaval.

Among the respondents, 6% Bodos said they had business partners who belonged to Adivasi community. Similarly 4% Adivasi's said they had business relationship with Bodos, 20% Bodo and 17% Adivasis voted for servant-master relationship. Again 60% Bodos and 61 % Adivasis said, they shared professional relationship in terms of land leasing. And the rest said that they shared a relationship of buyers and sellèrs. The following table reveals the state of professional relationship between the two groups in the post-conflict period.

Table 10: Inter-community professional relationship before conflict (in details)

Before	*Bodos* %	*Adivasis* %
Business partner	6	4
Master-servant relationship	20	17
Land leased-in and out and agricultural product	60	61
Buyer and seller	14	18
Total	100	100

After the conflict many changes in professional relationship between the two communities were noticed as reflected in the table below. As many as 54% of Bodo respondents and 72% Adivasis respondents said they share a relationship of buyers and sellers with each other. While there is a drastic drop in land lease-in and out relation that scared high in the pre-conflict situation, only 32% of Bodos and 15 % of Adivasis voted for this section. Similar change was noticed in the master-servant relationship between the two communities. Only 10% Bodos and 10% Adivasis said that they still share master-servant relationship.

Notably the change in professional relationship between the two groups has a close connection with the means of livelihood adopted by the groups in the post-conflict phase. After the conflict the Bodos showed less interest in establishing or re-establishing their professional ties with each other. Moreover, the lingering fear among majority of the Adivasis kept them away from initiating professional relationship with the Bodos. All these have a negative effect on the means of livelihood of the respondent. The following Table is in support of the above stated fact.

Table 11: Inter-community professional relationship after conflict (in details)

After	*Bodos* %	*Adivasis* %
Business partner	4	3
Master-servant relationship	10	10
Land leased-in and out and agricultural product	32	15
Buyer and seller	54	72
Total	100	100

Prior to the conflict 50% Adivasi and 49% Bodo respondents were engaged with farming. 11% Bodos and 3% Adivasis worked as wage earners while 10% Bodos and 8% Adivasis earned their livelihood from miscellaneous activities such as fishing, selling vegetables, etc. And the number of those who were unemployed stood at 30% Bodos and 39% Adivasis. However after the conflict (due to reasons stated above) rise in the number of unemployed was noticed. On the other hand there was a decrease (down to 25%) in the number of unemployment among the Bodos. While only 12% of Adivasi respondents said that they were engaged in farming (tilling others farms), the percentage of Bodos engaged in the same field stands at 55%. And 25% Adivasis said that in the absence of any permanent option of livelihood they earn their living by fishing, selling vegetables etc. In this same category the percentage of Bodo respondents stood at 10%. While 18% Adivasis and 10% of Bodos, were depended on daily wage.

Table 12: Professional engagement of Bodos and Adivasis before and after conflict

Before	*Communities*	
	Bodo %	*Adivasis %*
Farming	49	50
Wage earner	11	3
Fishing etc.	10	8
Unemployed	30	39
Total	100	100
After	*Bodo%*	*Adivasi %*
Farming	55	12
Wage earner	10	18
Fishing etc.	10	25
Unemployed	25	45
Total	100	100

Time is a great healer, but the case of BTAD is exception with no signs of healing, rather scars are left on the society with every passing moment. Waves of displacement have penetrated deep into the social fabric of the area so much so that it today has the potential of rekindling the underneath anger and frustration scraping away the inter-community trust. The sores are get to be healed even 10 years after the conflict.

Positive peace which goes beyond the absence of direct violence is holistic in nature. It needs to be supported by the process of reconciliation and justice. Under such circumstances it becomes essential to work out a reconciliation mechanism if one sincerely desires to give chance to positive peace. In addition to the tools suggested in the beginning of the chapter peace research expert Johan Galtung offers 12 approaches to reconciliation viz.

1) The exculpatory nature structure-culture approach
2) The reparation/restitution approach
3) The apology/ forgiveness approach
4) The theological/penitence approach
5) The juridical/punishment approach
6) The codependent origination/Karma approach
7) The historical/truth Commission approach
8) The theatrical/reliving approach
9) The joint sorrow/healing approach
10) The joint reconstruction approach
11) The joint conflict resolution approach
12) The ho'o ponopono approach.

It is easier to just lobby for reconciliation process than actually working on it. The complexities involved in bringing stubborn perpetrators and frustrated victims to talk tables at the same time are understandable. But we believe that perpetrators may become inflexible and victims at time may sound stubborn (they have every right to be so as they were at the receiving end) but there are still some mechanisms that can change the attitude of both the victims and perpetrators towards each other and help them to make a forward leap towards peace making. For instance reports and studies suggest that when the sufferings of the victims and their kith and kin gets official reorganization, they often become less reluctant in making peace with the perpetrators of conflicts.[4] Similarly, the involvement of a neutral third party having a thorough understanding of the local issues can persuade the perpetrators to change their rigid stand. Guided by our belief, impulsion and by the fact that reconciliation been a process requires serious engagement from civil society members we dared to apply some of the reconciliation approaches in BTAD. As expected our move was discouraged by all whom we visited, we made several calls to convince the need of such exercises. Discouragements came on our way in two forms – first form of discouragement came from that section whose members after much pursuance agreed to reveal the 'truth' about the conflicts but in separate sessions and not in the presence of 'the other group', while the other section discouraged us on the grounds that this process might rekindle inter-community conflict in the area. If we accepted any of the suggestions we would be jeopardizing the entire process before it started, but if we did not accept it the process would never start. Under such circumstances we were left with very few options, therefore we decided to go ahead with the reconciliation process but not in a large scale. It was decided that the process would start with grassroots level representatives and leaders belonging to the conflicting groups and considering the feedback from the exercise for future course of cotton.

Another matter of concern for us was the fact that in BTAD there is hardly any NGO or INGO seen as a neutral third party. As a result few steps taken by organizations such as Lutheran World Service India in the direction of reconciliation meet with little success. The prevailing situation in the area impelled us to take the challenge of applying some of the reconciliation approaches. Our only motto in so doing was to bring the conflicting parties to the talk table and find out the truth, and in this endeavor we took every possible step so as to ensure that we do not repeat past mistakes.

After a close examination of various reconciliation approaches we decided to make some variation keeping in mind local sensitiveness and resource constraints. Accordingly, a series of dialogue between the conflicting

parties were arranged at various levels. And representatives from students' organizations, women's organization, teachers, members of Sahitya Sabha, representatives from relief camps were invited to share their problems. In this section we put forth our findings of district level dialogue. In the beginning all the groups were given a chance to speak on the relation that they shared with one another prior to the conflict. In this context one of the women participants belonging to Adivasi community said, " prior to the conflict the relationship between Adivasis and the Bodos were very cordial." Another Adivasi participant in her mid 20s stressed that, "relation of my parents and grandparents with their Bodo neighbors and friends was more cordial compared to the relationship that I share with my Bodo friends and neighbors," rest of the members of her community nodded in agreement.

On the other hand members from the Bodo community, especially the youth, did not seemed to be comfortable talking much about the intercommunity conflicts. One of the participants Pratim Brahma Chaudhuri (name changed) registered his objection to the manner in which the two terms Bodos and non-Bodos are used. He said that "the expression conflict between Bodos and Non-Bodos is a very vague one. Bodos non- Bodo conflict suggests that the conflict was between Bodos and all other communities residing in BTAD, which is not the fact." However, history says the Bodo had clashed with Rajbongshis in 1989, the immigrant Muslims in 1993, and the Adivasis in 1996 and 1998. Moreover, other members from the Bodo community present in the meeting time and again insisted of having harmonious relationship with Adivasis. Additionally, other members of Bodo community were not willing to accept that (due to various unfortunate reasons) the community clashed with other inhabitants of the area. Some members of NGO too tried their best to support Brahma Chaudhuri. But there were strong protest against such claims by Bosco Chermako, Chief Organizing Secretary (Central Committee) of All Adivasi Students Association of Assam (AASAA). He alleged that "the Bodo leadership has only used the Adivasi community whenever required but never did anything for us." Substantiating his allegation he said "look at the EMs (pointing at the executive members of the Bodoland Territorial Council) we have only two representatives and they are merely 'puppets' in the hands of the other executive members."

The inmates from Bangaldoba part II relief camp Abdul Kuddus, Md. Hussain, Akbar Miya narrating the pangs of camp life, said: "we do not have enough to eat; only 10 days ration in a month is not enough. Most of the camp dwellers suffer from malaria, diarrhea, cold and fever. The government is still deceiving us."

To every allegation Pratim and his supporters had one reply: "The very concept of "Bodo- non-Bodo conflict" is a handiwork of mainstream intelligentsia."

However, every time the dialogue was about to take an unruly course some rational representatives belonging to both communities reminded the other members about the mission of this dialogue which helped them calm down to a certain extent.

A section of those who participated in the dialogue pointed out that had media been a little more responsible the magnitude of the problem would have been much less. Additionally, they also agreed that civil society was not doing much for reconciliation of the conflicting communities. While debate on who was responsible for the problem continued till the last participant left the meeting hall, and could not point out the exact causes, certain things were clear to us.

As the (first phase of) dialogue came to an end, certain things become clear:

- The tension between the conflicting communities is yet to be eased.
- A neutral third party intervention would provide both the parties an opportunity to discuss their issues.
- The success (read political success) of various movements such as the Assam Agitation and Bodo movement is a potential source of influence for other groups to mobilize individuals on ethnic lines with the ultimate intension of obtaining political power.
- Most importantly dialogue between the conflicting parties can become an important instrument through which the prevailing tension between the groups can be restrained to a considerable level. The potential of dialogue does not end here. From our experience in BTAD as well as other parts of the state and the region, we deeply feel issues concerning peace and conflict but many other socio-political rifts and crisis can be successfully dealt through engaging the stakeholders in meaningful dialogue(s).

At the end our heart was both happy and heavy. Happy because we could convince a section of the conflicting groups to come to the negatiation tables, heavy because we were not in a position to give a hearing to thousands of unheard voices and a great challenge awaits to convince all the sections of the conflicting parties to talk and free the area from the spell of palpable silence (absences of dialogue between the conflicting parties, the passive role of both intra-as well as inter-civil society members towards easing the tension between the conflicting communities in the area) that is so disturbing.

FOOTNOTES

1. Abu- Nimer, Mohammed, *Reconciliation, Justice, and Co-existence-Theory and Practice*, Lexington Books, 2001, USA, p.4.
2. Abu- Nimer, Mohammed, *Reconciliation, Justice, and Co-existence-Theory and Practice*, Lexington Books, 2001, USA.
3. Personal interview with president of Bangtol relief camp on 15.1.2008.
4. Supporting Justice, Co-existence and Reconciliation after Armed Conflict:Strategies for Dealing with the Past cited in http://www.berghof-handbook.net/uploads/download/theissen_handbook.pdf Accessed on 21.1.2010.

6

Conclusion

"Society is impossible without conflict. But society is worse than impossible without control of conflict."
—Paul Bohannan

We had no intention of just narrating the problem when we undertook the study. We applied all our experience and understanding of the situation to suggest some practical solutions for the problems discussed in the preceding chapters.

All facts and grievances aired during formal and informal meetings, compelled us to delve into some pertinent questions. *Where did things go wrong? What came between the dream of a greater Assamese society and its fulfillment? Why some communities once considered an integral part of the mainstream Assamese society, are asserting their aloofness today? Who will heal the social fractures—state, civil society or both? More importantly where to begin from?*

At this juncture the role of the state, in situations of conflict and thereafter, needs retrospection. So far, conflicts in India's northeast have been handled as merely law and order problem. The only answer that the state seems to have while dealing with the dynamic range of conflicts here is either by signing of ceasefire agreements or truce pacts. "Peace accords" are "signed between the state and its adversaries involved in some form of discord in an attempt to bring about "peace".[1] Such accords "can take many forms: from the minimal form of ceasefire agreement to the scope of a mini-constitution".[2] There are more than twenty active insurgent groups in Northeast and the Indian state has initiated and has signed agreements with half a dozen of them toward bringing pease in the region. Table 12 lists some of the important "peace efforts".

However, the outcome of these "peace accords" or to be more particular "peace attempts" has been anything but positive. As has been pointed out by John Lederach Paul, peace accords often become "an agreement that represents processes for continuing the conflict under new definitions".[3] Contrary to the genuine expectations that the "peace accords" will bring in peace, in many cases they have actually lead to newer conflicts. For instance, three accords (1949, 1960, and 1975) led to the creation of more rebel groups in Nagaland. Similarly, in our study area too Government of India (GoI) brokered two agreements with different Bodo groups. Though these agreements were designed to halt violence and usher in peace, the non-inclusion of all sections (read all communities) these accords would impact did not bring the desired change. In fact the non inclusive pre-agreement talks and sidelining of important stakeholders are often believed to be contributing towards the failure of the ultimate goal of the state- bringing peace in the area.

Table 12: Important peace agreements of Northeast India

Year	*Peace Accords / Ceasefire*	*Parties*
1986	Peace Accord	Union Government and Laldenga on behalf of Mizo National Front
1993	Bodo Accord	All Bodo Students Union and Assam Government.
1997	Bilateral Ceasefire	Government of India and National Socialist Council of Nagaland (NSCN-IM)
1998	Ceasefire	Government of India and National Socialist Council of Nagaland – Khaplang (NSCN-K)
2002	Ceasefire Agreement	United People's Democratic Solidarity (UPDS) with the Union Government of India
2003	Ceasefire Agreement	Dima Halam Daogah (DHD) leadership and the Union Government
2003	Memorandum of Settlement/Peace	Centre and the Bodo Liberation Tigers (BLT)
2005	Ceasefire Agreement	National Democratic Front of Bodoland (NDFB) with the Union Government of India

State has been using certain tools, that include ceasefire agreements, peace talks and accords for making peace. But peace has so far succeeded in eluding us all. The problem lies not with the aim but the means that has been adopted by the state in achieving peace. Peace talks and accords are viewed as end in themselves whereas in reality, for any of the "peace attempts" to succeed; they need to be viewed not as catalyst to further dialogues and discussions that could in course of time usher in sustained peace.

Increasing violent events in a nation that preached and taught lessons of non-violence and tolerance to the world leaves us pondering what went wrong. Many believe the development model of India to be faulty. In its pursuit to achieve an equal and justifiable society, the Indian state took certain balancing steps. In case of BTAD it was by including the Bodos of the area in the Sixth Schedule that the state tried to right the wrongs (perceived or real) done to them. However, in so doing it sowed the seeds of relative deprivation in the minds of the other communities residing in the area to whom the benefits of Sixth Schedule were not extended.

Additionally today, the democratic setup in India has been overpowered with manipulative political practices like endemic bad governance, institutional decay coupled with corruption at various levels, vote bank politics i.e., maintaining a loyal group of voters at any cost. All these factors have deprived a large section of people from the actual benefits of democracy. In other words an overwhelming section of people are being used in the name of democracy. One such section of people are the dwellers of the relief camps in BTAD for whom democracy starts and ends with the casting of vote, they are hardly aware that they also have the right to question their representative; that they have the right to make their dissatisfaction heard by casting no vote and still remain the citizen of the nation. It was found that for most of them the only reason for which they exercised their right to franchise was not because they expected their representatives to solve their problems but because they wanted to secure their names in the electoral rolls, in the absence of which they fear to lose the most authentic claims of citizenship.

If we judge democracy "not just by the institutions that formally exist but by the extent to which different voices from diverse sections of people can actually be heard"[4], then we can safely call the relief camps of BTAD 'undemocratic pockets' of world's largest democracy.

If state has failed to handle the situation aptly, members of civil society (i.e. non-state actors like NGOs, intelligentsia, literary organizations) are not flawless. Chowdhuri's repeatedly assertion that the very concept of "Bodo- non-Bodo conflict" is a handiwork of mainstream intelligentsia created with the intension of confusing others (here others mean those residing outside the state of Assam)," is a pointer that civil society's footsteps are no different from that of the state's. A large section of Bodos shares Chowdhuri's view. Mention may be made of the fact that at some point in time the problems faced by various tribes including the Bodos were not dealt sensibly by politicians or by the (mainstream) civil society. Hiren Gohain rightly pointed out that, "most of the industrial projects in the state after independence were granted land from the tribal belts and blocks, and "the evicted tribal peasants did not receive compensation even two decades after their eviction".[5] He further adds that "after Gopinath Bordoloi, the first chief minister of Assam, no other Assamese chief minister seems to have addressed the problem of tribal destitution...."[6] In addition to all these the tribals had to juggle to get employed. Other aspects like primary education, sanitation, etc., of them too lacked attention from the mainstream Assamese society. All these have perhaps left a lasting impact on the psyche of the Bodos the largest plain tribes of Assam especially the youth, as a result of which they seemed to need hardly any reason to air their grievance against the mainstream Assamese society.

Apart from the failure of the state, the civil societies of the conflicting communities have failed to make the most of their strength to avoid such a situation. Ashotoush Varshney pointed out that both intra-as well as inter-ethnic civil bodies play a crucial role in evading community conflicts. He also suggests a healthy, organized intra-ethnic civil association is a more effective safeguard against politics-driven ethnic polarization than every day inter-ethnic civil interactions. In the case of the Bodos and the Adivasis, the organized inter ethnic civil organizations were not sturdy enough to withstand the onslaught of disharmonizing factors that ultimately led to the ethnic conflict.[7]

Peace Prospects in BTAD

So far as our understanding goes there is an urgent need to go much beneath the surface, to unearth as to what went wrong among the conflicting communities. As with this study area, government has so far shown least interest in analyzing the reason(s) behind various other conflicts in the region. Without a comprehensive comprehension of the pre-conflict, conflict and post-conflict situation, resolving them merely through the application of "law and order" model looks a distant goal.

Besides analyzing the conflict, we also surveyed the NGOs, women organizations, and local clubs etc., in the BTAD area with an intention to identify some organizations that had the potential to work towards reviving the inter-community ties in the area.

To this end we traveled widely and visited 51 local organizations. *(Annexure III)*

The survey revealed the following:

Some prominent organizations such as All Bodo Women's

Welfare Federation (ABWWF), Bodo Sahitya Sabha (BSS), Action Network Trust (ANT), Lutheran World Service (LWS) and NEDAN Foundation have been operating in the study area for quite some time now. These organizations have undertaken various socio-economic activities for the welfare of the people in the area. However, unlike other parts of the world where NGOs and other organizations take up various activities with the objective of analyzing conflict and peace building, in the study area (like the rest of northeast) organizations of such kind are very limited. The terrains of peace building are still considered as difficult areas, hence maintaining a safe distance from the issue is a popular practice of NGOs in BTAD as well as in other conflict-affected areas of the region.

We also came across quite a number of *mahila samities* registered under the *Regulation of Society Act XXI 1860*. In Assam the existence of *mahila samities* dates back to the pre-independence era. The Dibrugarh Mahila Samiti, Tezpur Mahila Samiti, Nalbari Mahila Samiti had played a very important role in ushering in social changes. Some of these *samities* were actively involved in the freedom struggle. Their post-independence contribution towards the society continued in the form of support to social movement. Besides this *mahila samities* also took up social welfare activities and the issue of empowerment of women in particular. In BTAD too most of the villages surveyed, had one or more *mahila samities*. While some were functional, other were inactive but it was difficult for us to trace their executive members. However, some of the *samities* had their offices and official papers in place.

Experience gathered in the course of meeting these grassroots organizations revealed that lack of financial resources, lack of orientation programmes, leadership training coupled with decline in the overall activities of All Assam Pradishik Mahila Samiti that today concentrates mainly in major urban areas has effected the efficient functioning of *mahila samities* in the BTAD. The ABWWF which provide ample support to the Bodoland movement in various form, deserves mention. All Assam Tribal Women's Welfare Federation was rechristened ABWWF in 1993. Strongly believing in non-violence, it had condemned the Bodos-Adivasis clashes. Prominent member of the organization like Pramila Rani Brahma, Minister for Agriculture in the Government of Assam, visited the conflict affected areas and the relief camps and appealed for peace as well.[8] Besides, ABWWF has been running an orphanage called *Alayaran* since 2003. *Alayaran* houses 117 children, out of which 48 are girls. Most of these children have lost their parents in the ethnic clashes, factional clashes between rebel groups as well as witch-hunting. However, all the inmates of the orphanage belonged to the Bodo community. When we desired to learn what kept the organization from housing orphans from 'other communities', Kanan Basumatary, President, ABWWF Central Committee said that it becomes difficult for the workers of the organization (who are Bodos) to communicate with children belonging to other communities. The statement was loaded with subjectivity.

Mention may be made of *Adivasi Mahila Samity* that also played an active role immediately after conflict. Their activities included providing relief materials to the camp inmates and lobbying for better facilities in the camp for children and women. But unfortunately this organization, vibrant at one point of time, is almost in the state of defunct today. The All *Santhal Women Association* (ASWS) that came into existence on 8 March 2008 at Kasugaon is also worth a mention. This organization was formed by former as well as present relief camp dwellers. The president of the organization Sarojini Hasda said ASWS aims at spreading awareness on issues such need and necessity of education in the society in general and among the camp inmates in particular.

Going by history, activities and the enthusiasm of some of the mentioned organizations, Peace Studies strongly believes that if provided support and guidance they have the potential to bounce back to life. Since most of the *mahila samities* and other organizations visited are located in villages the task of maintaining peace at the grassroot level can begin with their initiative and sustained participation.

We further believe that *mahila samities* and local clubs are capable of organizing and involving the younger generations in various socio-economic activities such inter-village level youth camps, weaving, pottery, etc. These in future will open for them avenues of livelihood and also give the younger generation an opportunity to meet their peer groups belonging to other communities. In addition, sports and cultural events can become a viable media of bringing in peace.

During the course of the study, apart from empirical evidences we encountered with situations which time and again reconfirmed the fact that besides the direct victims of the conflict the younger generation harbours negative feelings against the 'other community'. For instance, Adivasi camp dwellers hesitated and in some cases they even refused to entertain our queries as one of our research team members belonged to the Bodo community. This and many such incidents made us come up with some ways to address the serious issue. After much pondering over the situation we feel that the problems of hostility, deep rooted hatred, fear, anger, biased views, stereotyping, lost empathy and compassion (of which BTAD seems to be a victim) that prevents communities and groups from achieving a just and durable peace, can be addressed by peace education. UNESCO Commission on Education in a 1996 report also emphasized on a type of education called "Learning to Live Together". Focusing on the usefulness of this approach towards making our only habitat, the earth more peaceful the report says,

> "by developing an understanding of others and their history, tradition and spiritual values and, on basis, creating a new spirit which, guided by recognition of our growing interdependence and a common analysis of the risks and challenges of the future, would induce people to implement common projects or to manage the inevitable conflict in an intelligent and peaceful way."

As school is an important agent of socialization, they can take up such activities so that the trend of socialization gets some positive boost. Education and training in peace can also help its learners to re-learn and solve problems without taking recourse to violence. Peace education will not only equip its learners with the capacity of reasoning vital for ending ongoing misunderstandings but can also reduce by several degrees the chance of future differences. The potentials of reasoning have been well expressed by Amartya Sen in the following lines:

> "Reasoning is a robust source of hope and confidence in a world darken by murky deeds—past and present. It is not hard to see why this is so. Even when we find something immediately upsetting, we can question that response and ask whether we should really be guided by it.
>
> Reasoning can be concerned with right way of viewing and treating other people, other cultures, other claims, and with examining different grounds for respect and tolerance. We can also reason about our own mistake and try to learn not to repeat them...."[9]

In addition to lessons on peace education that has the potential of challenging the ill effects of conflict, NGOs too can play a positive role in reviving the healthy socialization process that at one point of time glued the various communities of the area. Likewise, both state agencies and researchers need to realize and give due recognition to the fact that the gap between two is not helping anyone. Field findings need to be seriously examined while crafting policies. In simpler words, both policy makers and researchers have to give due respect and compliment each other. Moreover, it is in fact high time to remind ourselves that peace is a process that requires sustained attention from all – political parties in power as well as the signatories of the peace agreement besides a vigilant civil society.

FOOTNOTES

1. Das, Samir (2005), *Where Do The Autonomous Institution Come From*, in Samader,Ranbir(ed), *The Politics of Autonomy*, Sage Publication, New Delhi.
2. Swarna, Rajagopalan , *Peace Accords in Northeast India: Journey over Milestones*, East West Centre.
3. *Ibid.*
4. Sen, Amartya (2009), *The Idea of Justice*, Penguin Books, London, p.xiii.
5. Gohain, Hiren, "Ethnic Unrest in the North-East", *Economic and Political Weekly*, Vol.32, No.8 (Feb. 22-28, 1997), p.390.
6. *Ibid.*
7. Dutta, Anuradha, Sengupta, Urmimala, *Conflict amidst Diversity: Understanding the Bodo Milieu*, paper presented at national seminar organized by Dept. of Political Science, Gauhati University in collaboration with Indian Institute of Advanced Study, Shimla (February 29th to 2nd March, 2008).
8. Bhuyan Abhijit (2007), The Socio-Political Movement for Bodoland and Beyond, Peace Studies, Omeo Kumar Das Institute of Social Change and Development, Guwahati, pp.43-44.
9. Sen, Amartya (2009), *The India of Justice*, Penguin Books, New Delhi.

ANNEXURE I

BODO ACCORD

ALL BODO STUDENTS UNION AND GOVERNMENT OF INDIA MEMORANDUM OF SETTLEMENT, GUWAHATI

February, 20, 1993

The Memorandum of Settlement (MoS) on the fixed 'Bodoland' issue was signed. And with the signing of this MoS, the six-years old movement for a separate 'Bodoland' which started on March 2, 1987, also came to an end.

MEMORANDUM OF SETTLEMENT (BODO ACCORD)

1. Preamble

(i) Both the Government of India and the Government of Assam have been making earnest efforts to bring about an amicable solution to the problems of the Bodos and other Plains Tribals living in the north bank of river Brahmaputra within Assam.

(ii) Towards this end, the Government of India held a series of meeting with the State Government as well as with leaders of All Bodo Students' Union (ABSU) and Bodo People's Action Committee (BPAC). The State Government has also separately held discussions with the Bodo leaders. As a result, it has been considered necessary to set up an administrative authority within the State of Assam under a scheme, the details of which are outlined in the succeeding paragraphs.

2. Objective

The objective of this scheme is to provide maximum autonomy within the framework of the Constitution to the Bodo for social, economic, educational, ethnic and cultural advancement.

3(a) Name Bodoland Autonomous Council (BAC)

There shall be formed, by an Act of Assam Legislative Assembly, a Bodoland Autonomous Council (BAC) within the State of Assam comprising contiguous geographical areas between river Sankosh and Mazbat/ River Pasnoi. The land records authority of the State will scrutinize the list of villages furnished by ABSU/BPAC having 50 per cent and more of tribal population, which shall be included in the BAC. For the purpose of providing a contiguous area, even the villages having less than 50 percent population shall be included, BAC will also include Reserve Forest as per the guidelines laid by Ministry of Defence and Ministry of Environment and Forest Government of India, not otherwise required by the Government for manning the international border and tea gardens located completely within the BAC contiguous area.

(b) Powers

The BAC will comprise of a General Council comprising 40 members, 35 elected on the basis of adult suffrage and having a life of five years. The Government will have powers to nominate 5 members to the Council, particularly from groups, which could not otherwise be represented. This Council will have powers to make bye-laws, rules and orders for application within the BAC area on the subjects enumerated in Schedule 'A'.

(c) The executive authority of the BAC would be exercised in its Executive Body to be known as Bodoland Executive Council (BEC). The BEC will be responsible for implementation within the BAC area of the laws on subjects enumerated in Schedule 'A'.

(d) The General Council and the BEC will hold office during the pleasure of the Governor of Assam. Consultation with the State Law Department of Government of Assam would be necessary if the Governor proposed to dissolve either the General Council or the BEC before the expiry of its term in accordance with the provisions of law. The executive autority of its term in accordance with the provisions of law. The executive authority of the BEC will be exercised by the party enjoying a simple majority in the General Council. On completion of elections, the Governor would invite the leader of the majority party to constitute the BEC.

4. Finances

(i) (a) The finances for the BAC will be earmarked under a separate sub-head within the State budget, in keeping with the guideless laid down by the Government of India from time to time. The Government of Assam would have no powers to direct this earmarked allocation to other heads/areas except inexigencies when there is unavoided overall Budget cut.

(b) The provisions made in 4(i) (a) regarding allocation of funds should be in line with spirit of the Constitution (seventy second and seventy third) amendment.

(ii) The BAC would also receive grant-in-aid from time to time within the principles and policies enunciated by the Government of India.

(iii) The General Council will have powers to raise finances from levies/fees/taxes etc. on subjects mentioned in Schedule 'A' subject to Constitutional amendment mentioned above.

(iv) The finances for the BAC will be managed exclusively by its General Council and the statement of its annual audited accounts will be laid on the table of the State Assembly.

5. Powers of Appointments

The Bodoland Executive Committee would have powers to appoint Class -III and Class IV staff within its jurisdiction for implementation of schemes connected with the subjects enumerated in Schedule 'A'.

6. Reservation of Seats

The Election Commission of India will be requested by the BAC to consider seat reservation and delimitation of constituencies, both Lok Sabha and State Assembly, within the BAC area to the extent permitted by the Constitution and the law.

7. Special Provisions for the BAC Area

The General Council shall be consulted and its views shall be given due regard before any law made on the following subjects, is implemented in the BAC area:

(i) for religious or social practice of the Bodos,

(ii) the Bodo customary laws and procedures, and

(iii) The ownership and transfer of land within the BAC.

8. Special Status for the Bodoland Autonomous Council

The BAC shall, within the laws of the land, take steps to protect the demographic complexion of the areas falling within it jurisdiction.

9. Special Courts

Action will be taken in consultation with the Gauhati High Court to set up within BAC area Special Courts as specified below to try suits and cases between parties al of whom belong to Scheduled Tribe or Tribes in accordance with the tribal customary laws and procedure, if any:

(a) Village Courts,

(b) Subordinate District Customary law Courts within a civil Sub-Divisional Territory, and

(c) District Customary law Court.

10. Appointment in the Central Bodies

The claims of the Bodo shall be considered for appointment to the North-Eastern Council.

11. Official Language

The General Council can lay down policy with regard to use of Bodo language as medium of official correspondences within the BAC area. However, while correspondence will have to in bilingual form in accordance with the Article 345 of the Constitution and the provision of law in this behalf.

12. Changes in Geographical Boundary

The geographical area of the Bodoland Autonomous Council as agreed upon can be changed with the mutual consent of the BAC and the Government of Assam.

13. Revision of List of Scheduled Castes and Scheduled Tribes

The scheduling and re-scheduling of Scheduled Castes and Scheduled tribes residing within the Bodo areas will be done as per the Commission appointed by the Government of India under the Constitution.

14. Trade and Commerce

The General Council will have powers to regulate trade and commerce within its jurisdiction in accordance with the existing law. For this purpose, it can issue permits and license in individuals within the BAC area. The Government of Assam and the Union Government while considering allotment of permits to people residing within the BAC area will give preference to the Bodos.

15. Employment Opportunities

The BAC will have powers to reserve jobs for Scheduled tribes within its jurisdiction. However, exercise of such powers shall be in accordance with the existing constitutional and legal provisions.

16. Civil and Police Services

(i) The Government of Assam may from time to time post officers of the rank of Class –II and above to posts within the BAC in accordance with the exigencies. While making these postings due regard will be given to the views of BAC about officers being so posted.

(ii) The officers posted to the BAC area will be accountable to the BAC for their performance and the assessment of their work recorded by the BEC authorities, will be incorporated to their ACRs by the State Government.

(iii) The Central Government, while making recruitments from the State of Assam to the Army, paramilitary forces and police units, will hold special recruitment drives within the BAC area.

17. Appointment of Interim Bodoland Executive Council

The Government of Assam will take steps for the formation of an Interim Bodoland Executive Council for the BAC from amongst the leaders of the present Bodoland movement who are signatories to this settlement, during the transition period, i.e prior to the holding of elections. Such Interim Council would be formed before a prescribed date mutually agreed between the Central and State Governments.

18. Relief and Rehabilitation

(i) ABSU-BPAC leaders will take immediate steps to bring overground and deposit with the District authorities all arms, ammunition and explosives in the possession of their own supporters and will co-operate with the administration in bringing overground all Bodo militants along with their arms and ammunition etc. within one month of the formation of the Interim BEC. In order to ensure the smooth return to civil life of the cadre and to assist in the quick restoration of peace and normalcy, such surrenders made voluntarily will not attract prosecution.

(ii) The Government of Assam will consider sympathetically the withdrawal of all cases against persons connected with the Bodoland Movement excluding those relating to heinous crimes.

(iii) The Government of India will initiate steps for review of action against the Bodo employees of Government of India and subordinate offices as well as in respect of Central Government Undertakings. Similar action would be taken by the Government of Assam.

(iv) The Government of Assam will initiate immediate steps for suitable rehabilitation of the Bodo militants coming overground as a result of this settlement. Similarly, the Government will organize exgratia payments as per rules to next of the kins killed during the Bodo agitation.

19. Share in Collection of Excise Duty on the Tea

The Government of Assam will deposit in the BAC Fund revenue collected from the tea gardens falling within the BAC area.

20. Protection of Rights of Non-Tribals

The Government of Assam and the BAC will jointly ensure that all rights and interests of the non-tribals as on date living in BAC area in matters pertaining to land as well as their language are protected.

21. Ad-hoc Central Grant for launching the BAC

After the signing of this settlement, an ad-hoc Budget on reasonable basis will be prepared by Interim BEC and discussed with the State and Central Governments for necessary financial support.

Sd/-
(K.S. RAO)
Addl. Chief Secretary to the Government of Assam

Sd/- S.K. Biswamutiary
President, ABSU

Sd/ Rabi Ram Brahma
General Secretary, ABSU
Sd/- Subhash Basumatari
Chairman, BPAC

In the presence of

Sd/- Rajesh Pilot
Ministery of State (Internal Security)
Ministry of Home Affairs
Government of India.

Sd/- Hiteswar Saikia
Chief Minister of
Assam State Govt.
Assam

APPENDIX 'A'

List of Subjects and Departments over which BAC will have Control within the BAC Area

1. Cottage Industry
2. Animal Husbandry and Veterinary
3. Forests
4. Agriculture
5. PWD
6. Sericulture
7. Education
   (a) Adult Education
   (b) Primary Education
   (c) Upto Higher Secondary including vocational training
8. Cultural Affairs
9. Soil Conservation
10. Co-operation
11. Fisheries
12. Panchayat and rural development
13. Handloom and textiles
14. Health and Family Welfare
15. Public Health Engineering
16. Irrigation
17. Social Welfare
18. Flood Control schemes for protection of villages (not of highly technical nature)

19. Sports and Youth Welfare
20. Weights and Measures
21. Library Services
22. Museums and Archaeology
23. Urban Development – Town and Country Planning
24. Tribal Research Institute
25. College Education (General)
26. Land and Revenue
27. Publicity/Public Relations
28. Printing and Stationary
29. Tourism
30. Transport
31. Any other matter connected with development
32. Municipal Corporation, Improvement Trusts, District Boards and other local authorities
33. Tribal Welfare
34. Markets and Fairs
35. Lottereis, Theatres, Dramatic performance and Cinemas
36. Vital Statistics including registration of births and deaths
37. Food and Civil Supply
38. Intoxicating liquors, opium and derivatives etc.

ANNEXURE II

Memorandum of Settlement on Bodoland Territorial Council (BTC)

On February 10, 2003, the Assam government, the Union government and the Bodo Liberation Tigers signed the Memorandum of Settlement on Bodoland Territorial Council (BTC), *in New Delhi. The jurisdiction of the BTC shall extend over 3082 villages and the BTC has been given legislative powers over 40 subjects. The accord provides for an Executive Council comprising of a maximum of 12 Executive Members, including a Chief and a Deputy Chief, with adequate representation to the non-tribal population.*

1. The Government of India and the Government of Assam have been making concerted efforts to fulfil the aspirations of the Bodo people relating to their cultural identity, language, education and economic development. Towards this end, a series of talks were held between Government of India, Government of Assam and Bodo Liberation Tigers (BLT) since March, 2000. As a result, it is agreed to create a self-governing body for the Bodo Areas in the State of Assam as follows:

2. Objectives

The objectives of the agreement are: to create an Autonomous self governing body to be known as Bodoland Territorial Council (BTC) within the State of Assam and to provide constitutional protection under Sixth Schedule to the said Autonomous Body; to fulfil economic, educational and linguistic aspirations and the preservation of land-rights, socio-cultural and ethnic identity of the Bodos; and speed up the infrastructure development in BTC area.

3. Area

3.1. The area of proposed BTC shall comprise all the 3082 villages and areas to be so notified by the State

Government. The above mentioned villages and areas shall be divided into 4 contiguous districts after reorganisation of the existing districts of Assam within a period of 6 months of the signing of the agreement on the lines of the proposal given by BLT subject to clearance of the Delimitation Commission.

3.2 A committee comprising one representative each from Governments of India & Assam and BLT will decide by consensus on the inclusion of additional villages and areas in the BTC from out of 95 villages and areas on the basis of the criteria of tribal population being not less than 50%, contiguity or any other agreed relevant criteria within a period of three months of signing of this MoS.

4. Status of Bodoland Territorial Council

The provision of the Sixth Schedule and other relevant Articles of the Constitution of India will apply to BTC, *mutatis mutandis* in terms of this agreement. The safeguards/ modifications for the non-tribals in BTC area, inter-alia, will include the following:

4.1. Provision of para1(2) of Sixth Schedule regarding Autonomous Regions will not be applicable to BTC.

4.2. A provision will be made in para 2(1) of the Sixth Schedule for increasing the number of members for BTC up to 46 out of which 30 will be reserved for Scheduled Tribes, 5 for non-tribal communities, 5 open for all communities and 6 to be nominated by Governor of Assam from the unrepresented communities for BTC area of which atleast two should be women. Nominated members will have the same rights and privileges as other members, including voting rights. Election from the 40 constituencies of BTC shall be on the basis of adult franchise. The term of the elected members of BTC shall be for 5 years.

4.3. Safeguards for the settlement rights, transfer and inheritance of property etc. of non-tribals will be suitably incorporated in para 3 of the Sixth Schedule. Any such law as may be made by the BTC in this regard will not, in particular:

(a) Extinguish the rights and privileges enjoyed by an citizen of India in respect of their land at the commencement of BTC, and

(b) Bar any citizen from acquiring land either by way of inheritance, allotment, settlement or by way of transfer if such citizens were eligible for such bonafide acquisition of land within the BTC area.

4.4. Provision will be added in para 6 of Sixth Schedule that in BTC area, language and medium of instruction in educational institutions will not be changed without approval of the State Government.

4.5. Provision of para 8 of Sixth Schedule regarding power to assess and collect land revenue and impose taxes shall be applicable to BTC.

4.6. Para 10 of the Sixth Schedule will not be applicable to BTC area.

4.7. Provision of Article 332(6) of the Constitution will be so modified that the existing status of representation of BTC area in the State Assembly is kept intact. After the creation of BTC, the Parliamentary & Assembly Constituencies shall be delimited by the Delimitation Commission in accordance with the provisions of the Constitution.

4.8. In the event, **Panchayati Raj** system ceases to be in force in the council area, the powers of the

Panchayati Raj Institutions in such matters shall be vested with the Council.

The Amendments to the Sixth Schedule shall include provisions in such a manner that non-tribals are not disadvantaged in relation to the rights enjoyed by them at the commencement of BTC and their rights and privileges including land rights are fully protected.

5. Power and Functions

5.1. The Council shall have legislative powers in respect to subjects transferred to it as enumerated below. All laws made under this paragraph shall be submitted forthwith to the Governor and until assented to by him, shall have no effect. The BTC shall have executive, administrative and financial powers in respect of subjects transferred to it.

Subjects to be entrusted to BTC by Assam Government

1. Small, Cottage and Rural Industry; 2. Animal Husbandry & Veterinary; 3. Forest; 4. Agriculture; 5. PWD; 6. Sericulture; 7. Education (Primary Education, Higher Secondary Including vocational training, Adult Education, College Education (General); 8. Cultural Affairs; 9. Soil Conservation; 10. Co-operation; 11. Fisheries; 12. Panchayat and Rural Development; 13. Handloom and Textile; 14. Health & Family Welfare; 15. Public Health Engineering; 16. Irrigation; 17. Social Welfare; 18. Flood Control; 19. Sports & Youth Welfare; 20. Weights and Measures; 21. Library Services; 22. Museum & Archaeology; 23. Urban Development – Town and Country Planning; 24. Tribal Research Institute; 25. Land & Revenue; 26. Publicity/Public Relations; 27. Printing & Stationery; 28. Tourism; 29. Transport; 30. Planning and Development; 31. Municipal Corporation, Improvement Trust, District Boards and other local

authorities; 32. Welfare of Plain Tribes and Backward Classes; 33. Markets and fairs; 34. Lotteries, Theatres, Dramatic performance and cinema; 35. Statistics; 36. Food and Civil supply; 37. Intoxicating liquors, opium and derivatives etc.; 38. Labour and employment; 39. Relief and Rehabilitation; 40. Registration of Births and Deaths.

5.2. There shall be an Executive Council comprising of not more than 12 Executive Members, one of whom shall be the Chief and another one the Deputy Chief of the said Executive Council. There shall be adequate representation for the non-tribal members in the Executive Council. The Chief and the Deputy Chief of the Council shall have the status equivalent to the Cabinet Minister and the other Executive Members equivalent to the Minister of the State of Assam for protocol purposes in BTC area.

5.3. The BTC shall have the full control over the officers and staff connected with the delegated subjects working in the BTC area and shall be competent to transfer officers and staff within the BTC area. ACRs of these officers shall also be written by the appropriated BTC authority.

5.4. BTC shall also be competent to make appointments for all posts under its control in accordance with the rules of appointment followed by the Government of Assam. However, the posts, where recruitment is made on the recommendation of APSC, shall not be covered under this provision. The Council may constitute a Selection Board for appointments to be made by it and may also make rules, with the approval of the Governor of Assam to regulate appointments and to ensure adequate representation for all communities living in the Council area.

5.5. No posts shall be created by BTC without concurrence of the Government of Assam and it shall also abide by the decision of the Government of Assam in respect of abolition of/temporarily keeping vacant any post.

5.6. Development functions and bodies within the competence of BTC shall be transferred to BTC. In respect of DRDA, concurrence of Government of India will be obtained.

5.7. The offices of the Dy. Commissioner and Superintendent of Police will be outside the superintendence and control of BTC.

5.8. The State Government would provide an amount, to be decided every year on population ratio basis, as grants-in-aid in two equal instalments to the BTC for executing development works. The proportionate share for the BTC shall be calculated on the basis of the plan funds available after setting aside the funds required for earmarked sectors and the salary. This amount may be reduced proportionately if the state plan allocation is reduced or there is plan cut due to resource problem. In addition, the Council will be paid a suitable amount of plan funds and non-plan funds to cover the office expenses and the salaries of the staff working under their control. The BTC shall disburse the salaries of the staff under their control and would ensure strict economy in the matter.

5.9. BTC authority shall prepare a plan with the amounts likely to be available for development works, both under State share and Central share, covering any or all the activities of the departments under their control. The Council shall have full discretion in selecting the activities and choosing the amount for the investment under the same in any year covering all groups of people in a fair and equitable manner. This plan will be a sub set of the State plan and would be treated as its integral part. Once the plan of the State, including BTC plan, gets the approval of the Planning Commission the BTC authority will start execution of their plan in the BTC area. Modifications, if any, made by the Planning Commission in the BTC proposal, shall be binding on the BTC authority. The State Government shall not divert the funds allocated to the BTC to other heads and also ensure its timely release. BTC may have Planning Department to prepare the plans for BTC area to be submitted to Planning Commission through the Government of Assam.

5.10. The executive functions of the BTC shall be exercised through its Principal Secretary who shall be an officer of the rank not below of Commissioner/ Secretary to Government of Assam. The sanctioning powers of the Government of Assam shall be vested with the Principal Secretary of BTC and sanctioning powers of head(s) of the Department(s) including for technical sanction shall be conferred on the senor most officer of that Department preferably not below the rank of Additional Director, who may be designated as Director of BTC for that department. The Principal Secretary and other officers shall exercise their powers under the overall guidance and supervision of BTC.

6. Law and Order

To strengthen the Police Administration, Government of Assam shall appoint an IGP for 4 districts of BTC and the jurisdiction of the DIG Kokrajhar shall also be modified to cover these 4 districts.

7. Revision of list of ST

Consequent to the inclusion of BTC area into the Sixth Schedule, the list of ST for the State of Assam shall be so modified so as to ensure that the tribal status of Bodos and other tribals living outside the BTC are does not get affected adversely.

8. Grant of ST status of Bodo Kacharis of Karbi Anglong and NC Hills Districts

The Government of India agrees to consider sympathetically the inclusion of the Bodo Kacharis living in Karbi Anglong and NC Hills Autonomous Council area in the ST (Hill) List of State of Assam.

9. Development of Bodo Language

9.1. The Government of India agrees to consider favourably the inclusion of Bodo Language in Devnagri Script in the Eighth Schedule of the Constitution.

9.2. Bodo language shall be the official language of BTC subject to the condition that Assamese and English shall also continue to be used for official purpose.

10. Additional Development Package for BTC

10.1. The State Government, within the limitation of financial and other constraints, may offer or allow the Council to offer, possible and sustainable additional incentives for attracting private investment in the Council area and would also support projects for external funding.

10.2. In order to accelerate the development of the region and to meet the aspirations of the people, the Government of India will provide financial assistance of Rs 100 crores per annum for 5 years for projects to develop the socioeconomic infrastructure in BTC areas over and above the normal plan assistance to the State of Assam. The size of the Corpus will be reviewed after a period of 5 years. Suitable mechanism will be built in the system to ensure that the funds are transferred to BTC in time and at regular intervals. An illustrative list of projects which may be considered to be taken up in BTC given below:

List of projects

1. To establish a centre for development and research of Bodo language; 2. Upgradation of existing educational infrastructure by way of renovation/addition of buildings, providing modern facilities for teaching such as computers, science laboratories etc. from primary level to college level in BTC area; 3. A cultural complex to be established at Kokrajhar to promote and develop Bodo tradition and cultural heritage; 4. To establish a super-speciality hospital with all modern facilities at Kokrajhar Government Hospitals shall be established in all district, sub-divisional and block headquarter; 5. To establish sports complexes in all the district headquarters; 6. Food processing plants and clod storage facilities at Kokrajhar, Kajolgaon, Udalguri and Tamulpur; 7. Construction of a bridge over river Aai to connect Koilamoila, Amguri etc. with the rest of the district; 8. To build a Bodoland Bhawan in Delhi; 9. To set up integrated agro-processing park and textile-cum-apparel park; 10. Revitalisation of Kokilabari Agricultural Farm; 11. To develop adequate infrastructure to promote Manas Sanctuary as an international tourist spot; 12. To complete Champa, Suklai and Dhansiri irrigation projects; 13. To construct a highway on the Indo-Bhutan border from Jamduar to Bhairabkunda to connect remote places located adjacent to the border; 14. To set up model dairy, fishery, horticulture and poultry farms/training centres at

different places in all the 4 districts to encourage youth for self-employment; 15. To enhance the existing facilities in veterinary hospitals in BTC area.

10.3. Government of India will provide necessary one time financial assistance required for development of administrative infrastructure in the newly created district headquarters, sub-divisional headquarters and book headquarters, besides the BTC Secretariat Complex at Kokrajhar

11. Centrally funded University

11.1. A centrally funded Central Institute of Technology (CIT) will be set up to impact education in various technological/vocational disciplines such as Information Technology, Bio-Technology, Food Processing, Rural Industries, Business Management, etc.

11.2. The CIT will be subsequently upgraded to a Centrally funded State University with technical and non-technical disciplines to be run by the BTC.

12. Relief & Rehabilitation

12.1. The BLT would join the national mainstream and shun the path of violence in the interest of peace and development. After the formation of the interim council of BTC, BLT will dissolve itself as an organisation and surrender with arms within a week of swearing-in of the interim council. The State Government would provide full support to relief and rehabilitation of the members of BLT who would surrender with arms in this process in accordance with the existing policy of the State. Financial support in such cases, however shall be limited to be provisions of the scheme prepared and funded by the Government of India. Withdrawal of cases against such persons and those related to overground Bodo movement since 1987 shall be considered according to the existing policy of the State of Assam.

12.2. The Government of India will initiate steps for review of action against the Bodo employees of Government of India and subordinate officers as well as in respect of Central Government Undertakings. Similar action would be taken by the Government of Assam.

12.3. Bodo youth will be considered for recruitment in Police, Army and Paramilitary forces to increase their representation in these forces.

13. Special Rehabilitation Programme for the people affected by ethnic disturbances:

The Special Rehabilitation Programme (SRP) for the people affected by ethnic disturbances in Assam, who are at present living at relief camps in Kokrajhar, Bongaigaon etc. shall be completed by the Government of Assam with active support of BTC. Necessary funds for their rehabilitation shall be provided by the Government of India and lands which are free from all encumbrances required for such rehabilitation shall be made available by the BTC.

14. Interim Council

Immediately after signing of the agreement, Interim Executive Council for BTC shall be formed by Governor of Assam from amongst the leaders of the present Bodo movement, including the signatories to this settlement, and shall include adequate representation to the non-tribal communities in BTC area. The Interim Council shall not continue for a period beyond 6 months during which period election to the Council shall be held. Government of Assam shall dissolve the Bodoland Autonomous Council (BAC) and repeal the BAC Act.

15. Government of Assam will consider inclusion of all tribals including Bodos in RHAC/MAC/LAC in consultation with leaders of these Councils.

16. The Implementation of the provision of the Memorandum of Settlement shall be periodically reviewed by a Committee comprising representatives of Government of India, Government of Assam and BTC.

Signed on 10th February, 2003 at New Delhi in the presence of Shri L.K. Advani, Hon'ble Deputy Prime Minister of India and Shri Tarun Gogoi, Chief Minister of Assam.

(Hagrama Basumatary) Chairman Bodo Liberation Tigers (P K Dutta) Chief Secretary Govt. of Assam (R C A Jain) Secretary (BM) Ministry of Home Affairs Government of India

ANNEXURE III

List of the Organizations visited/contacted by the research team

Sl. No.	*Name of the Organization*	*Persons met/ President or Secretary*	*Place*
	1	*2*	*3*
1.	Tamulpur Anchalik Gramdan Sangha	Rabin Upadhay	Tamulpur, Baska
2.	Green Rural Development Society	Chandan Kr. Sama	Barkhopa, Tamulpur
3.	Social Empowerment and Development Organization	Michael Hansda	Sashipur, Darangamela, Tamulpur, Baska
4.	Community Welfare and Development Centre	Properteen Basumatary	Kokrajhar
5.	Bodoland Life Establishment Society	Pranjit Boro	Ronsaidhang, Basugaon, Chirang
6.	Centre for Youth and Rural Development	Dominik Basumatary	Bangtol, Chirang
7.	Green Live NGO	Honokanta Basumatary	Kokrajhar
8.	Discovery Club	Bishnu Brahma	Kokrajhar
9.	DRISTI – Dimalu Rural Institute of Social Trust and Implementation	Ronondra Narzary	Gossaigaon, Kokrajhar
10.	Bodhiaguri Santhal Cultural Group	Philip Murmu	Kokrajhar

(Contd...)

	1	*2*	*3*
11.	District Development Organization		Basugaon, Kokrajhar
12.	Rural Unemployment Youth Development Association Society	Sanjay Brahma	Kochugaon, Kokrajhar
13.	Anjali Sukati SHG Foundation	Jammuna Basumatary	Kokrajhar
14.	Centre for Voluntary Services and Development	Ilas Basumatary	Runikhata, Kokrajhar
15.	Lafa Saikho Social Service Society	Pritam Brahma Choudhury	Kokrajhar
16.	Sabkata Judasik Club	Could not contact	Sabkata, Gossaigaon
17.	Rajbanshi Kolabari Mahila Samity	Smt. Kanaklata Roy	Kokrajhar
18.	Naraya Narayan Club	Avinash Rai	Santhaibari Romoni Ashrom, Dotma
19.	Lakhimi Socio-Economic Development Society	Could not contact	Ghogmari, Baksa
20.	Community based Development Society of Kamrup	-do-	Dhulabari, Deulkuchi, Baksa
21.	Sadou BAC School Siksha Matri Kendriya Committee	-do-	Barama, Baksa
22.	North East Research & Social Work Networking	-do-	Near Law College, Kokrajhar

(Contd...)

	1	2	3
23.	North East Swrang Afat (NESA)	-do-	Kumarikata, Baksa
24.	Manab Sewa Mahila Committee	-do-	Baksa
25.	Jagaran Gramin Vikas Society	-do-	Dongpar, Nagrijuli, Baksa
26.	Sewa NGO	-do-	Kumarikata, Baksa
27.	Himalaya NGO	-do-	Jalah, Baksa
28.	The Action North-East Trust (ANT)	Dr. Sunil Kaal	BOC Gate, Bongaigaon
29.	Initiative for Development (IDEA)	Samkhan Brahma	Bongaigaon, Chirang
30.	Oritha Human Services	Ananta Ramchiary	Barama, Baksa
31.	Manas Sousi Konkor	Bijoy Choudhury	Subankhata, Baksa
32.	NEDAN Foundation	Digambar Narzary	Baganshali, Kokrajhar
33.	Bodo Sahitya Sabha	Brojendra Kr. Brahma	
34.	Bishmuri Anjaloo Club cum Library	Jaimanta Mosahary	Bishmuri, Kokrajhar
35.	Madhuchakra Development Organization	Pijush Barman	Basugaon, Chirang
36.	SERHDO (NGO)	Suniram Hasda	Borjhara, Salakati, Kokrajhar

(Contd...)

	1	*2*	*3*
37.	Socio-Economical Rural Health & Development Organisation	Thakur Hasda, Sahar Hazarika	Barjhora, Salakati, Kokrajhar
38.	No. 2 Goladangi Mahila Samity	Somasti Basumatary	Goladangi, Gossaigaon, Kokrajhar
39.	Tulshibil Mahamaya Library-cum-Club	Bikram Narzary	Tulshibil, Kokrajhar
40.	Garlabari Gwjwnshri Youth Club & Library	Hakim Bargayary	Bishmuri, Kokrajhar
41.	No. 3 Rajapara Hirimbha Mohila Samity	Anjali Brahma, Promila Brahma	Gossaigaon, Kokrajhar
42.	No. 2 Dawaguri Mahila Samity	Romoni Basumatary	Simaltapu, Gossaigaon, Kokrajhar
43.	Haraputa Telipara Mahila Samity	Rekharani Dey	Haraputa, Gossaigaon, Kokrajhar
44.	Labrabati Purnima Mahila Samity	Rohini Basumatary	Patgaon, Kokrajhar
45.	Babubil (College Para) Mahila Samity	Pujari Kachari	Gossaigaon, Kokrajhar
46.	No. 1 Bajugaon Mahila Samity	Rina Basumatary	Gossaigaon, Kokrajhar
47.	Green Rural Development Society	Chandan Kumar Sarma	Barkhopa, Tamulpur, Baksa
48.	Baraja Bathou Ashram	Baneswar Narzary	Jamguri, Hajaragaon, Baksa

(Contd...)

	1	*2*	*3*
49.	Socio-Eco-Educational Agricultural and Health Development Organization	Amlesh Brahma	Goreswar, Tamulpur, Baksa
50.	Gariyoshi Gramya Vikash Parishad	Could not contact	Charaimari, Baksa
51.	Adivasi mahila samity	Sukumari Haasda (ex-secretary)	Gossaigaon

Bibliography

Barman, Prateeti, Local Self-Governance, Civil Society, and Peace Prospect: A Case Study of Nalbari District, Assam, OKDISCD, Guwahati, 2005

Barpujari, H.K, *North-East India: Problems, Policies, and Prospects: Since Independence*, Spectrum Publication, 1998

_______ *Problem of the Hill Tribes: North-East Frontier*, Lawyers Book Stall, Gauhati, 1970

Baruah, Sanjib (ed.), *Beyond Counter-Insurgency: Breaking the Impasse in Northeast India*, Oxford University Press, *New Delhi,* 2009

_______, Immigration, Ethnic Conflict and Political Turmoil: Assam 1979-1985, *Asian Survey*, vol. 26, November 11, 1986

_______, Postfrontier Blues: Toward a New Policy Framework for Northeast India, *Policy Studies 33,* East- West Center Washington, 2007

Bhaumik, Subir, "Troubled Periphery: Crisis of India's North East," Sage Publication, New Delhi, 2009

Bhuyan, Abhijit, 2006, "Gandhian Non-Violence as a Means of Dispute Settlement in Assam: A Case Study of

Tamulpur Anchalik Gramdan Sangh, Kumarikata", Peace Studies, OKDISCD, Guwahati

Chandoke, Neera, *The Conceits of Civil Society*, Oxford University Press, New Delhi, 2003

Choudhury, Sujit, *The Bodos: Emergence and Assertion of an Ethnic Minority,* Indian Institute of Advanced Studies, Shimla, 2007

Das, Samir Kumar, *Blisters on their Feet: Tales of Internally Displaced Persons in India's North East*, Sage, New Delhi, 2008

Deowri, Indibor, "Jangosthi Samasya Atit, Bartaman Bhabisyat", *Journal Emporium,* Nalbari, 2001

Dutta, Anuradha, Bhuyan, Ratna (ed.), *Genesis of Conflict and Peace*, Akansha Publishing House, New Delhi, 2007

Das, Samir Kumar, "Conflict and Peace in India's Northeast: The Role of Civil Society", *Policy Studies 42,* East- West Center, Washington, 2007,

_______, "Where Do The Autonomous Institutions Come From?" in Samaddar, Ranbir (ed) *The Politics of Autonomy*, Sage Publications India Pvt. Ltd., New Delhi, 2005

______, *Peace Processes and Peace Accords*, Sage Publications India Pvt. Ltd., New Delhi, 2005

Elliott, Carolyn M, *Civil Society and Democracy: A Reader*, Oxford University Press, New Delhi, 2003

Gohain, Hiren, in Reflection on Ethnicity and Ethnic Movement, in Deka, K.M. & Phukan, K.N.(ed) "Ethnicity in Assam", Centre for North-East Studies, Dibrugarh, 2001

Goswami, Triveni, "Role of Women as Peace Builders With Special Reference to Nagaland", Peace Studies, Omeo

Kumar Das Institute of Social Change and Development, Guwahati, Assam, 2006

Hussain, Monirul, "State Identity Movements and Internal Displacement in the North-East India", *Economic and Political Weekly*, December 16, 2000

_____ *Interrogating Development: State, Displacement and Popular Resistance in North East India*, Sage Publication, New Delhi, 2008

Jeong, Ho-Won, *Understanding Conflicts and Conflict Analysis*, Sage Publication, New Delhi, 2008

Junne,Gerd, and Verkoren, Willemijin (ed), *Postconflict Development: Meeting New Challenges*, Viva Books, New Delhi, 2006

Manchanda, Rita, Ambivalent Gains in South Asian Conflicts, in Meintjes, Sheila etal. (eds) *The Aftermath: Women in Post-Conflict Transformation*, Zed Books, London, 2001

Melander, Erilk, et.al, *How to conduct a conflict analysis* published by Sida, 2004

Mishra,Udoyan, *Nation Building and Development in North East India*, Purbanchal Prakashan, Guwahati,1991

_______ *Periphery Strikes Back: Challenges to the Nation-State in Assam and Nagaland*, Indian Institute of Advanced Studies, 2000

Parikh, Sunita, "Religion, Reservation and Riot", in Basu, Amrita (ed), Kohli, Atul (ed), *"Community Conflicts and the state in India"*, Oxford University Press, New Delhi, 1998

Prabhakaran, M.S., "Bodos Hopes, Harsh Realities," *The Hindu*, October 4, 1990

________, "The Northeast Turmoil," *The Hindu*, October

________, "Manufacturing Identities?" *Frontline*, Vol. 22-Issue 20, Sep 24-Oct 07, 2005

Roy, Ramashray, Miri, Sujata, Goswami, Sandhya, *Northeast India,* Anshah Publishing House, New Delhi, 2007

Saikia, Jaydeep, *Frontiers in Flames: North-East India in Turmoil*, Viking, New Delhi, 2007

Sen, Amartya, *The Idea of Justice,* Penguin Books, London, 2009

Swarna, Rajagopalan , *Peace Accords in Northeast India: Journey over Milestones*, East West Center.

Tarabout, Gilles, and Samaddar, Ranbir, "Conflict, Power and the Landscape of Constitutionalism, Routledge, 2008

Tongeren van, Paul, et al. (ed.), *People Building Peace II Successful Stories of Civil Society*, Viva Books Private Limited, 2007, New Delhi

Websites

http://www.jstor.org/

http://www.iansa.org/women/documents/women_armed_conflict.pdf http://www.unesco.org/new/en/unesco/

http://en.wikipedia.org/wiki/Bodoland

Index